Edmund Phelps • Hian Teck Hoon
Gylfi Zoega

The Great Economic Slowdown

How Narrowed Technical Progress Brought Static Wages, Sky-High Wealth, and Much Discontent

palgrave
macmillan

Edmund Phelps
Columbia University
New York, NY, USA

Hian Teck Hoon
Singapore Management University
Singapore, Singapore

Gylfi Zoega
Department of Economics
University of Iceland
Reykjavik, Iceland

ISBN 978-3-031-31440-7 ISBN 978-3-031-31441-4 (eBook)
https://doi.org/10.1007/978-3-031-31441-4

This Palgrave Macmillan imprint is published by the registered company Springer Nature Switzerland AG.
The registered company address is: Gewerbestrasse 11, 6330 Cham, Switzerland

Preface

Much discontent has arisen over the past several decades in the West. In the labor force, there is a sense among many people of not getting ahead—not noticeably, at any rate—and a heightened resentment over the wage gains made by some others. Household surveys have shown that job satisfaction has fallen far below what it was five decades ago.

We contend that this dissatisfaction with jobs is not only due to wages—in absolute or relative terms. Economies in the West increasingly fail to provide the kind of challenging, purposeful work that for many people is central to the good life. Adding to the discontent among many in recent decades is the huge rise of wealth among many shareowners and corporate executives. Moreover, the downward slide of the yields on savings and retirement funds has dimmed hopes of accumulating enough wealth for greater security. Where these dissatisfactions are rife, there is a dissatisfied society. Yet not much has been understood about the unrelenting *causes* of these developments.

The challenge we have taken up in this book has been to determine whether established economics—in particular, neoclassical theory—can explain these unprecedented developments in the West's economies. Our hypothesis is that these socioeconomic setbacks are the immediate effects of the huge loss of technical progress that set in some fifty years ago. This book, drawing on roots and extensions of existing macroeconomic theory, aims to *identify* and *quantify* the economic and societal impacts of the historic slowdown of technical progress in the West that began in the early 1970s and, after the decade-long Information Revolution, resumed after the turn of the century. This slowdown in innovation explains stagnant wages, rising inequality, declines in job satisfaction, meager rates of return to investment, the effects on the real value of existing government debt, and the effects on real prices of assets from houses to shares.

Social discontent arises from many factors, for sure. Some of them have nothing to do with the economy. But we believe that the decline in innovation deserves more attention. A dynamic economy delivers jobs that allow workers to exercise skills and creativity that in turn contributes to well-being. A sclerotic economy not only lowers productivity and wages but deprives workers at all income levels these intangible rewards. These themes, as well as a thesis on the wellsprings of a dynamic economy, are developed in Phelps's book *Mass Flourishing* and tested in our book *Dynamism*.

Remarkably, in all this time, rather little work, theoretical as well as econometric, has been done to estimate the wide range of effects the Western slowdown has had on the economy—and thus on society. Nor is there a theoretical model derivable from intertemporal theory, microeconomic and macroeconomic, on which such an econometric model could be based. So teachers of economics will welcome the derivation of such a theory-based model. Many economists will also want to think about the empirical significance of the econometric results—results coming from tectonic shifts in the parameters of the model especially around the early 1970s. Our econometric model is important for understanding the parametric shifts in those years.

At another level, the results are also informative in indicating that the parameters of the model being estimated have been affected by historic shifts. It seems likely that these parameters have been tossed up or down more than once as the forces in society have pushed and pulled them over the centuries. The ideas that govern society have been tossed about, and our econometric estimations are snapshots of sometimes shifting and always evolving society.

In this book, we also provide a theoretical framework with which to study the effects of increased public debt on the path of the economy—on wealth, consumption, real interest rates, investment, and economic growth. We introduce too the effect of slower population growth and some forces coming from the rest of the world—in particular, the rise of China's economy.

New York, NY, USA — Edmund Phelps
Singapore, Singapore — Hian Teck Hoon
Reykjavik, Iceland — Gylfi Zoega

Acknowledgments

We are grateful to Professor Ron Smith, Birkbeck College, and Professor Richard Robb, Columbia University, for their comments and advice.

CONTENTS

About the Authors

Edmund Phelps *the 2006 Nobel Laureate in Economics, is McVickar Professor Emeritus of Political Economy and director of the Center on Capitalism and Society at Columbia University. His work can be seen as a lifelong project to put "people as we know them" into economic theory. In Mass Flourishing (2013) and Dynamism (2020), he argues and tests that broad job satisfaction in a nation requires widespread, indigenous innovating and that depends on the nation's values. His latest book is My Journeys in Economic Theory (2023).*

Hian Teck Hoon *is Professor of Economics at the Singapore Management University. He is a co-author of Dynamism: The Values That Drive Innovation, Job Satisfaction, and Economic Growth (2020). He is the author of Trade, Jobs and Wages (2000) and Economic Dynamism, Openness, and Inclusion: How Singapore Can Make the Transition from an Era of Catch-up Growth to Life in a Mature Economy (2019). Hian Teck is a past vice-president of the Economic Society of Singapore (2002–2004).*

Gylfi Zoega *is Professor of Economics at the University of Iceland and (now part-time) at Birkbeck College, London, since 1993 and was an external member of the Monetary Policy Committee of the Central Bank of Iceland from 2009 to 2023. His research is focused on saving, financial stability and growth, including the financial crisis in Iceland starting in 2008. He co-authored the book Dynamism and co-edited Preludes to the Icelandic Financial Crisis (2011), The 2008 Global Financial Crisis in Retrospect (2019) and Fault Lines After COVID-19: Global Economic Challenges and Opportunities (2023).*

List of Figures

List of Tables

Introduction

We extend macroeconomic theory to analyze the effects of two forces acting on the economy in its many dimensions: the great slowdown of technical progress and the huge increase of public debt. The results of an economy's operation, however—especially the operation of an "advanced economy" such as that found in the West—cannot be reduced to the path of wage rates or wage incomes. Such an economy generates a complex of results: effects on capital, wealth, share prices, and interest rates, as well as on wage rates and job satisfaction. A long, unexpected decline in rates of return on savings and retirement funds may cause anxiety, and a long rise in share prices and wealth may add to demoralization among those seriously lacking in shareholdings and other wealth.

Yet there has been little agreement over what has brought on that slowdown. In our main model, the prime causal force is technological progress: the ups and downs in the growth rate of total factor productivity—not labor productivity alone or capital productivity alone—although other causal forces such as demographic change and some public policy shifts will be added. In the one-sector version, consumer goods and investment goods are produced with the same capital-labor ratio; in the two-sector version, labor produces the investment good, and capital produces the consumer good. After setting out two versions of such a model, we proceed to make statistical estimates of the economic power of the various causal forces in the model driving up or down the chief variables of the model: labor participation, capital accumulation, and wealth level, as well as wages, share prices, the share of profits in GDP, and real interest rates.

A central part of the work, then, is its attention to the long-term effects of policy moves, not just the near-term effects that are of such keen interest to politicians. We use our theoretical framework to study the effect of an increase in public debt on the path of the economy.

The theoretical frameworks used in this book are close relatives of those used in our book *Structural Slumps* (1994). This does not mean that this book is similar at every point in *Structural Slumps* on the causes of the swings in unemployment in the West—in particular, the high unemployment of the 1980s and 1990s. The real rate of interest was a major element of *Structural Slumps* as well as in this book—so was the wage rate—but of course, those variables surely figure in every existing intertemporal model, from Fisher to Hicks. We have benefitted from revisiting *Structural Slumps* on occasion.

Stylized Facts

We start by looking at the data on total factor productivity growth. The slowdown in the rate of productivity growth is visible in Table 1, which shows average decadal productivity growth over the past century.

We note the rapid growth in productivity in war-torn Europe in the 1950s, 1960s, and 1970s, and in Japan as well. Productivity growth then slowed down considerably in these countries in the 1980s and 1990s. By contrast, in the US, UK, and Canada we see a slowdown in the 1970s, and then, in the US, a temporary pickup in the 1990s.

During the prewar period, productivity growth was strong in Continental European countries in the 1920s and, in Germany, in the 1930s as well. In the US it was weaker in the 1920s—although our data show years of swift productivity growth within the decade—but stronger in the 1930s. During the 1930s, productivity growth was faster in the US than in the other countries, apart from Germany.

In the chapters that follow, we show how a slowdown in productivity growth may cause equilibrium real interest rates to fall. Table 2 shows the nominal yield on ten-year government bonds in the G7.

While high nominal interest rates in the 1970s and the 1980s were in large part due to inflation and high central bank interest rates intended to curb inflation, we can compare nominal rates in the two decades following the Second World War and the last two decades. Interest rates are higher in the postwar decades than in the past two decades. The same pattern can

Table 1 Productivity (TFP) growth (%) by decade for G7

	1920–29	*1930–39*	*1940–49*	*1950–59*	*1960–69*	*1970–79*	*1980–89*	*1990–99*	*2000–09*	*2010–19*
Canada	2.2	-0.4	4.5	2.3	2.1	0.8	0.2	0.8	0.3	0.6
France	7.1	0.2	0.6	4.4	4.0	2.6	1.8	1.0	0.5	0.6
Germany	2.6	3.0	-3.0	5.1	3.3	2.7	1.5	1.8	0.3	1.1
Italy	2.4	0.2	1.1	4.4	4.7	2.6	1.1	0.8	-0.5	0.2
Japan	1.2	2.1	-3.4	5.0	5.5	2.1	2.2	-0.2	0.0	0.7
UK	1.8	0.2	2.3	1.1	2.1	1.8	1.7	1.6	0.8	0.5
US	1.0	2.1	3.0	2.5	2.1	0.9	0.9	1.5	1.0	0.9

Source: Bergeaud et al. (2022)

Table 2 Long-run nominal interest rates (%) by decade for G7

	1920–29	*1930–39*	*1940–49*	*1950–59*	*1960–69*	*1970–79*	*1980–89*	*1990–99*	*2000–09*	*2010–19*
Canada	5.1	3.9	2.9	3.7	5.7	8.5	11.7	7.9	4.9	2.4
France	5.2	4.0	4.0	6.8	6.5	9.1	11.8	7.0	4.3	1.6
Germany	7.3	6.3	4.7	5.8	6.6	7.9	7.6	6.6	4.1	1.1
Italy	6.2	6.0	6.2	6.2	6.3	10.9	14.8	10.0	4.5	3.2
Japan	6.4	7.9	4.0	6.0	6.8	7.7	6.5	3.6	1.4	0.5
UK	4.6	3.5	3.1	4.3	6.6	11.8	10.4	8.0	4.7	2.5
US	3.9	2.9	2.3	3.0	4.7	7.5	10.6	6.7	4.5	2.4

Source: Jorda-Schularick-Taylor macro-history database

be seen from the early 1990s for real interest rates in Table 3. This decline in interest rates coincides with the decline in productivity growth shown in Table 1.

The decline in productivity growth and real interest rates coincides with a rise in public debt in the 1980s, 1990s, and the past two decades, as is shown in Table 4.

Tables 5 and 6 show the average level of investment as a ratio to GDP and the share of profits in GDP, respectively.

The share of investment in GDP has declined since the 1960s and 1970s in Europe and Japan. As Table 6 indicates, it is noteworthy that the ratio of profits to GDP has increased in the US and Canada since the 1970s.

Summary of Our Models

We interpret historical events using three aggregative models: a one-sector neoclassical model, a two-sector Austrian model, and the Phelps and Winter (1970) customer-market model (as well as variations of these models).

A standard formulation of the one-sector model relies on an aggregative neoclassical production function. In this model, to satisfy a set of stylized facts along a balanced-growth path, technical progress has typically been assumed to be entirely labor-augmenting, so that we can speak of variables, such as capital, as being expressed per effective worker. Along a balanced-growth path, real wages grow at the rate of growth of labor-augmenting technical progress and the real interest rate is constant.

The one-sector model incorporates Blanchard's perpetual youth concept: that is, individuals face a constant death rate over their finite lives. They are born without any assets but save and accumulate assets over their lives. Consumption depends on their human capital—calculated as the present discounted value of future wages—and their stock of nonhuman wealth. Firms rent the services of labor and capital from households, and both wages and the rental on capital are determined in competitive factor markets. The equilibrium real rate of interest is the one that equalizes the supply of saving (coming from households) with the demand for capital (coming from firms).

The Austrian model is a special case of the two-sector model in which only labor is required to produce the pure investment good, and only capital is required to produce the pure consumption good. There is a labor-augmenting technology that grows exogenously, boosting the productivity of the investment-good sector. We can, however, introduce a

Table 3 Long-run real interest rates (%) by decade for G7

	1920–29	*1930–39*	*1940–49*	*1950–59*	*1960–69*	*1970–79*	*1980–89*	*1990–99*	*2000–09*	*2010–19*
Canada	6.3	6.1	-1.5	1.4	3.1	1.4	5.2	5.6	2.7	0.7
France	-1.4	2.8	-17.5	0.8	2.6	0.5	4.5	5.0	2.4	0.4
Germany	-13.5	8.7	-0.2	4.7	4.1	3.0	4.6	4.1	2.5	-0.2
Italy	2.0	6.2	-17.8	3.3	2.7	-0.4	4.0	5.7	2.2	2.0
Japan	8.4	6.8	-22.8	3.3	1.5	-0.6	3.9	2.3	1.7	0.0
UK	7.4	3.9	-2.8	-0.2	3.2	0.6	4.1	4.6	2.8	0.3
US	4.4	5.4	-3.1	1.3	2.3	0.8	5.4	4.0	1.9	0.6

Source: Jorda-Schularick-Taylor macro-history database

Table 4 Government debt to GDP ratio (%) by decade for G7

	1920–29	*1930–39*	*1940–49*	*1950–59*	*1960–69*	*1970–79*	*1980–89*	*1990–99*	*2000–09*	*2010–19*
Canada	64.3	94.2	117.9	69.3	62.1	51.1	61.8	92.8	75.7	88.7
France	183.2	132.0	44.3	33.8	19.9	17.3	29.3	51.9	67.0	94.2
Germany	20.7	38.5	121.0	20.9	18.8	22.3	37.7	51.0	63.8	71.8
Italy	124.5	96.0	67.2	32.1	30.3	49.4	73.3	108.2	102.9	128.4
Japan	33.6	61.3	81.8	11.3	7.0	23.6	63.6	91.3	170.7	231.3
UK	175.2	173.8	201.1	161.7	99.9	55.3	44.0	41.2	43.4	85.4
US	23.6	35.5	80.7	68.6	46.3	34.5	41.7	61.7	62.3	102.0

Source: Jorda-Schularick-Taylor macro-history database

Table 5 Investment-to-GDP ratio (%) by decade for G7

	1920–29	*1930–39*	*1940–49*	*1950–59*	*1960–69*	*1970–79*	*1980–89*	*1990–99*	*2000–09*	*2010–19*
Canada	16.8	10.0	13.0	23.3	22.2	22.8	22.6	20.3	22.1	23.5
France	21.1	25.8	19.3	28.8	25.3	27.0	23.2	21.3	21.7	22.6
Germany	15.0	12.0	20.5	23.6	27.8	25.4	22.6	24.1	20.5	20.4
Italy	12.4	15.0	13.4	22.9	24.8	25.2	23.1	20.0	21.0	18.0
Japan	18.3	14.1	18.6	22.3	31.9	33.1	29.2	28.7	22.9	21.9
UK	8.9	9.6	6.7	13.7	19.4	22.2	22.0	20.7	18.1	16.8
US	14.2	7.8	10.9	20.3	19.7	19.7	20.1	20.6	21.8	19.5

Source: Jorda-Schularick-Taylor macro-history database

Table 6 Ratio of profits to GDP (%) for G7

	1950–59	*1960–69*	*1970–79*	*1980–89*	*1990–99*	*2000–09*	*2010–19*
Canada	–	–	34.8	37.1	35.5	39.1	38.6
France	41.7	38.3	34.9	33.7	35.7	35.7	34.7
Germany	–	–	36.3	36.6	38.5	39.8	38.6
Italy	–	–	47.4	50.5	50.1	49.5	47.6
Japan	–	–	49.4	44.8	43.5	44.3	43.0
UK	–	–	41.0	43.4	43.2	39.3	39.5
US	–	–	34.8	36.4	36.6	38.3	40.8

Source: Eeckhout (2022a, 2022b)

parameter that augments capital used in the consumption-good sector that sometimes experiences a level increase, thereby boosting the productivity level of the consumption-good sector. Along a balanced-growth path, the physical capital stock grows at the rate of labor-augmenting technical progress, and the relative price of the investment good measured in units of the consumer good, which is also the shadow value attached to a unit of physical capital, is proportional to the productivity level of capital in the consumption-good sector. The output of the investment good, as well as the consumer good, grows at the sum of the growth rate of the labor force and the rate of growth of labor-augmenting technical progress. The real interest rate is constant along a balanced-growth path, and the real wage grows at the rate of growth of labor-augmenting technical progress. The share of labor in national income is also constant in steady state.

The Phelps-Winter customer market model features an endogenous price-marginal cost markup. Due to the sluggish flow of information, the firm possesses some transient monopoly power at each moment. If it raises its price, it does not instantaneously lose all its customers; nor does it gain the whole market instantly if it cuts its price. A reduction in markups is an investment in new customers, which in a symmetric equilibrium only ends up in lower prices without any one firm increasing its market share. It follows that in a symmetric equilibrium the market share of each of the identical firms is unchanged over time, but markups change in response to other economic variables. Thus, in this model, the customer is an asset.

We can incorporate labor-leisure choices into the one-sector model, as well as in the Austrian model. This enables us to connect TFP growth to employment via wages and wealth from the labor supply side and via the shadow price of physical capital from the labor demand side. The theory of labor supply is consistent with the fact that even as the real wage increases at, say, two percent, total wealth is also growing at two percent in the long run so that employment is constant. As wealth is constantly increasing, people are constantly tending to switch to unpaid work or work with shorter hours unless firms make wage offers that keep rising to counterbalance that tendency. What matters for employment is the wage relative to wealth. The increase in household wealth will reduce labor supply—it raises the wage required by workers so that it contracts or lowers employment and pushes up wages. An exogenous shift in preferences that raise the required wage has similar effects on employment and wages.

Finally, we model the world of two economies with a shared capital market where one country has a lower rate of time preference than the other—alternatively, a lower rate of population growth. In autarky, the interest rate is higher in the country with a higher rate of time preference—which we take to be the US—than the one with a lower rate of time preference—which we take to be China. With free international capital mobility, there are capital inflows into the US, which becomes the international net debtor, and the world interest rate is somewhere between the autarkic interest rates of the debtor and creditor countries. Compared to autarky, there is more capital in the US and less in China. The capital flows reduce net wealth in the debtor country but increase it in the creditor country. In essence, the creditor country has extended its ownership of capital located in its own country through the bond market to include capital located in the debtor country. With more capital situated in the debtor country, real wages are higher than in autarky, while the real wage in the creditor country falls.

This suggests that there is more capital in the US and less in China because of the downward effect of China's surplus capital on equilibrium interest rates in the US. Perhaps more surprisingly, real wages are higher in the US because of the capital inflow from China, in contrast to conventional wisdom about the negative effect of China on employment in the US. A lower rate of population growth in China has a similar effect. It follows that countries with low rates of population growth become net creditors and countries with faster population growth net debtors.

We now come to the last model used in this book: the Nelson-Phelps (1966) model. In the global economy, in which national economies are open to new developments elsewhere, indigenous innovation can take place in one country, and its ideas can be adopted in another. Catch-up through adoption of foreign technology by technological followers can lead to rapid growth initially, but that growth tapers off as these economies approach their steady-state technological gaps. An example is Japan's strong growth from 1950 to 1990. The rapid growth of China since 1978 is a more recent example. We show how a slowdown in the West affects technological followers and the productivity gap between the two.

Consequences of the Slowdown

Consider an unanticipated decrease in the rate of growth of labor-augmenting technical progress. In the one-sector model, this leads to capital deepening—due to increased saving by workers whose human capital has fallen due to weaker anticipated wage growth—that is, capital per effective worker increases and the real interest rate decreases. Although the movement along the factor-price frontier implies that the real wage per effective worker is increased, (unnormalized) real wages now grow at a slower rate.

In the Austrian model, an unanticipated decrease in the rate of growth of labor-augmenting technical progress results in real wages growing at a slower rate and the shadow value of physical capital rising because the whole term structure of interest rates is shifted downwards. In one variation of the Austrian model, we suppose that the consumption-good sector is a customer market. We show how an unanticipated decrease in the rate of growth of labor-augmenting technical progress can raise markups when the marginal value of customers to the firm falls, reducing the marginal cost of raising markups. The fall in the value of a customer is caused by expectations of weaker growth in consumption due to diminished productivity growth. Interest rates fall by less than productivity growth because a rise in the shadow prices of capital raises consumption demand.

The Increase of Public Debt

Suppose that there is a helicopter drop of government debt in the one-sector model. The government levies a tax to service the debt, but there are no other public expenditures. Because households have finite lives, the helicopter drop of debt increases household wealth even though households must pay taxes to service the debt. While households perceive the debt to be a form of wealth, the government debt is not productive from the standpoint of the economy and creates a wedge between the supply of wealth and the demand for capital. In the new equilibrium, real interest rates are higher, the stock of capital is lower, and household wealth exceeds capital used in production.

In the Austrian two-sector model with an investment good and a consumer-goods sector where labor produces capital and capital produces the consumer good, the induced increase in consumption demand cannot be met by increased production of the consumer good given the current stock of capital. The only way the excess demand for the consumer good can be eliminated is via a drop in the real price of the investment good caused by a rise in the real rate of interest. As in the Stolper-Samuelson theorem, the factor used intensively in the production of capital, which is labor, sees its remuneration fall. With endogenous labor supply, employment decreases.

In the customer-market model, a helicopter drop of public debt raises current consumption demand, which increases the marginal benefit of raising markups while lowering the value of customers due to higher real interest rates, thus reducing the marginal cost of raising prices. The customer market model also generates insights about the welfare effects of public debt. While increased public debt can be shown to crowd out the physical capital stock, there is the question of whether the level of capital exceeds the golden rule capital stock. In the two-sector model with customer markets, the shadow price of capital is the discounted stream of future marginal product of capital, but only after taking into account the markup, which reduces the share of marginal product going to the owners of capital in the form of rental.

This relates directly to the golden rule of Phelps (1961), since the markup of price over marginal cost creates a wedge between the rental of capital—the sum of the real interest rate and the rate of depreciation—and the rate of return to capital. The higher the markup is, the lower the real rate of interest for a given rate of return to capital. Therefore, a low real rate of interest does not have to imply dynamic inefficiency, and increased public debt may lower output and consumption even when real interest rates are close to zero.

We can sum up the effect of increased public debt in a closed economy as follows. The increased debt raises the real rate of interest, lowers the real wages, and crowds out part of the capital stock in addition to raising markups of price over marginal cost and the share of profits in national output.

We can also show the effect of increased debt in a two-country model. When public debt is introduced in the two-country model—inhabited by the US and China—in the indebted US, capital flows from China to the

US, driving the world real interest rate higher and reducing the stock of capital in both countries. When the US increases its level of public debt, the effect is to increase household wealth in that country, which raises consumption and the equilibrium real rate of interest. This causes a further capital flow from the creditor country, and the world real interest rate rises. The net effect is to lower the stock of capital in both countries and to make the debtor country more indebted to the creditor country while, paradoxically, making households in the debtor country feel wealthier due to the failure of Ricardian equivalence.

References

Bergeaud, A., Cette, G., & Lecat, R. (2022, November 24). *The long-term productivity database*. Prod. Bank of France. http://www.longtermproductivity.com/about.html

Eeckhout, J. (2022a, October 31). *The profit paradox: How thriving firms threaten the future of work*. https://www.theprofitparadox.com/

Eeckhout, J. (2022b). *The profit paradox: How thriving firms threaten the future of work*. Princeton, NJ: Princeton University Press.

Nelson, R. R., & Phelps, E. S. (1966). Investment in humans, technological diffusion, and economic growth. *American Economic Review, 56*(1/2), 69–75.

Phelps, E. S. (1961). The golden rule of accumulation: A fable for growthmen. *American Economic Review, 51*(4), 638–643.

Phelps, E. S. (1994). *Structural slumps: The modern equilibrium theory of unemployment, interest and assets*. Cambridge, MA: Harvard University Press.

Phelps, E., & Winter, S. G. Jr. (1970). Optimal price policy under atomistic competition. In E. S. Phelps et al., *Microeconomic foundations of employment and inflation theory*. New York: Norton.

CHAPTER 1

Innovation

We have to start with innovation and growth. Since its founding in 2001, the Center of Capitalism and Society at Columbia University has organized studies and conferences on the nature and causes of productivity growth. We were convinced that the treatment of growth in mainstream literature called for improvements. In the Solow growth model, productivity growth falls like manna from heaven, while in the "endogenous-growth" literature of Romer and Aghion and Howitt, firms invest in new technologies, which turn out to be successful with fixed probabilities. We depart from this treatment by assuming, or rather realizing, that innovation occurs under conditions of uncertainty in the Knightian sense. There is no way a firm or an individual can calculate a priori the probability of success. Instead, firms exist and operate in uncertainty about the consequences of current actions.

Preceding the endogenous-growth literature and the seminal contribution of Solow are Schumpeter and Hayek, but they also looked past the role of uncertainty. In the Schumpeterian model of innovation, the sole task of the entrepreneur is to bring new technologies to the market. Scientists make discoveries, and the entrepreneurs create the consumer products that use the new technologies. The entrepreneur invests in new inputs or introduces new varieties of outputs, which free the economy from diminishing returns on capital and enable it to sustain constant growth of its production possibilities.

E. Phelps et al., *The Great Economic Slowdown*, https://doi.org/10.1007/978-3-031-31441-4_1

The Hayekian entrepreneur is closer to the Center's way of thinking about growth. Information is dispersed across individuals and firms, and each of them has insights about what works and what does not work. These insights guide business decisions: new products are introduced based on existing technologies. We can think of the Hayekian entrepreneur as bringing the economy closer to its productivity frontier. However, although he faces genuine uncertainty in his decisions, this is not explicitly acknowledged.

Our approach goes beyond that of Schumpeter and Hayek by realizing that all people—not just scientists and entrepreneurs—are capable of having original ideas, and some of these ideas have commercial applications. In every firm there is staff working in management, production, or even distribution, and they are all capable of having new ideas about how to improve the performance of the firm.

Humans are more complicated creatures than the profit-maximizing or cost-minimizing firm in neoclassical economics or the Schumpeterian entrepreneur in endogenous-growth models. Edmund Phelps has argued in his book *Mass Flourishing* that people in varying degrees possess creativity and derive satisfaction not only from consuming and enjoying leisure but also from having new ideas—especially ideas for new things such as new products and new ways of producing. In the nineteenth century this kind of ***indigenous innovation*** sprung up in much of the West. Owing to its failure to recognize innovation of this kind, the standard theory finds it difficult to explain intercountry differences in the rate of growth or why a period of rapid growth—such as the European Golden Age in the 1950s, 1960s, and 1970s—comes to an end. But it has other weaknesses also: in particular, it ignores sources of life satisfaction other than consumption and leisure; for instance, the job satisfaction that comes from a stimulating work environment. Our approach, instead, emphasizes the sources of life satisfaction and explains differences in growth across countries in terms of how receptive societies are to ordinary people innovating in different spheres of life. We also consider that there may be multiple impediments to innovation in the workplace: for example, regulations and red tape, and vested interests and rent-seeking by employees, managers, and owners.

In *Mass Flourishing,* Phelps describes the excitement that arose in the West as new ideas exploded, and for a great many people work shifted increasingly from being routine to being engaging and challenging. The book describes the unprecedented dynamism within the people. Businesspeople noticed unexploited opportunities to produce existing products in a more efficient way, and workers spotted or conceived of better ways to do their job or organize their work. The result was not a trading economy like those in Medieval Venice, Florence, and Genoa, but an economy of innovation, which pulled out the productivity frontier.

Our model of indigenous innovation can be described with three equations. The first equation shows output (Y) as a function of the number of ideas (I) in existence and the share of the labor force producing output ($1 - \zeta$). The ideas have either been generated indigenously (I) or adopted from other countries (I^*).

$$Y_t = F\left(I_t, I_t^*, 1-\zeta\right), F_1 > 0, F_2 > 0, F_3 > 0 \tag{1.1}$$

The people working in the production sector must screen and assess the ideas that exist and also implement them. The model of Nelson and Phelps (1966) shows how a level of training or education is helpful to workers when they select and implement ideas. There is also indigenous innovation, which is generated in the home country by a fraction ζ of the labor force, making the number of ideas grow over time.

$$dI_t / dt = G\left(I_t, I_t^*, \zeta\right), G_1 > 0, G_2 > 0, G_3 > 0 \tag{1.2}$$

Here the existing indigenous ideas I and imported ideas I^* help generate more indigenous ideas. The heartbeat of a capitalistic economy is in the generation of new ideas that can increase productivity over time. These include the reorganization of production, the use of new or better inputs, the elimination of jobs through the use of new technologies, such as artificial intelligence, and so on. Both the rate at which new ideas are created and the share of the labor force doing the inventing depend on the values and attitudes of the population. We explore this in greater depth later.

In small countries, imported or adopted ideas from other countries are important. The flow of ideas coming from abroad is exogenous at rate λ and reflects how innovative the rest of the world is.

$$dI_t^* / dt = \lambda \tag{1.3}$$

We have used this framework to explain differences in the rate of growth of output across countries, and also possible reasons for the acceleration of productivity growth such as that occurring during the European Golden Age, and deceleration such as occurred in the 1970s and 1980s.

The determinants of growth in our framework include values, the financial system, the system of regulations and red tape, and the education and ability of managers to learn about and choose from among different inputs and technologies, to name a few causal factors. A good economy is a dynamic one that is receptive to new ideas, where people gain satisfaction from innovating and employers are willing to listen to their ideas, where businesspeople seek out new opportunities, and where there is a financial system that is able to select good business ideas and fund them. There is also the ability to learn about new technologies and business ideas from abroad, as is described by Nelson and Phelps (1966), and the ability of firms within a country to learn from the leading firm. Finally, a dynamic economy has what Amar Bhidé called "venturesome consumers," by which he meant both consumers who are willing and able to use new products and technologies and firms that take advantage of research and innovation taking place in other countries.[1] Examples abound. The aircraft manufacturer Boeing assembles its Dreamliner passenger jet using components from all over the world. Where Boeing is concerned, the dynamism of the American economy is to a large extent its ability to take advantage of technologies discovered in other countries. The same applies to the Apple iPad and iPhone, assembled in China using technology not only from the US but also from Asia and Europe.

Many factors can hamper this kind of innovative economy. Vested interests can impinge on the adoption of new or foreign technologies through a protective regulatory framework. The financial system may support prevailing industries and business practices instead of innovation, and corporatist industrial policies may hinder change and creative destruction.

A top-down system of economic governance is detrimental to indigenous innovation. This applies to communism, of course, but also to its twentieth-century rival system, corporatism. Corporatism, created at the end of the nineteenth century as an alternative to both capitalism and communism, proposed centralized planning, the unity of the nation, and the coordination of the government, employers, and unions. The first economy to be organized in a corporatist manner was Italy under

[1] See Bhidé (2010).

Mussolini. Juan Peron's Argentina tried to emulate Mussolini's system in the 1940s and the early 1950s with catastrophic consequences.[2]

Several corporatist institutions found in today's world deter innovation. There is employment protection, which makes it difficult for firms to reorganize and trim their workforce. This has the direct effect of making firms hesitate before hiring new workers or setting up new operations. It also makes it more difficult to innovate because employment protection is effectively a tax on the hiring and firing of labor. Only when an innovator overcomes the Knightian uncertainty that he faces can he justify hiring new workers, but employment protection may then prevent him from doing so, putting sand in the wheel of the capitalist system. Employment protection also reduces mobility between declining and rising industries. Moreover, in a corporatist economy, a government may decide to subsidize declining industries to protect jobs and keep them alive while taxing expanding firms. Yet another corporatist institution is excessive red tape; that is, regulations and licenses that obstruct new firms and new projects. Red tape also cuts into job creation and the formation of new businesses. Labor unions may have similar effects. The inflation tax is used to fund spending, which is geared toward the redistribution of income, and the tax system is structured to extract resources from some industries for the benefit of others. Finally, tariffs lower the volume of trade.

A country's institutions reflect and interact with a nation's values, the set of attitudes and beliefs that guide people in the workplace. In the recently published book *Dynamism*, we found that productivity growth, job satisfaction, employment, and labor force participation are positively related across countries to values that parents instill in their children. In countries where parents teach children to follow rules and obey authorities, the economy performs worse, and in countries where parents teach children to be independent, it performs better. We find in *Dynamism* that well performing countries include the US; the Nordic countries of Denmark, Finland, and Sweden; and Ireland, the UK, and Australia. Following them are the large continental economies of France, Germany, Italy, and Spain, which lag in terms of performance and values. Greece is close to the bottom of the group.

[2] More distant ideological relatives of Mussolini were Spain's Francisco Franco and Portugal's António Salazar. In spite of the failure of corporatism in these countries, many corporatist institutions still exist in Europe and, especially, in South America.

In a study of European regions published in *Capitalism and Society*, Arnorsson and Zoega (2016) show, using European regional data, that teaching children to be independent, imaginative, and tolerant contributes positively to social capital, as does trust toward fellow citizens. There are also differences in the attitude of adults toward work. They assign different importance to work, job security, job initiative, and achieving on the job. These differences can explain in a statistical sense the difference in unemployment, male labor force participation, and average hours of work across European (NUTS 1) regions.[3]

We are left with explaining the epochs of high and low growth rates. Why did Western Europe and Japan grow rapidly in the 1950s, 1960s, and 1970s, and why did this growth subsequently peter out? The most obvious answer is the same as the one that explains the rapid growth in Eastern Europe in the past 20 or so years and the very rapid growth in China since the early 1990s. It goes back to Nelson and Phelps (1966): for an underdeveloped country, foreign technology is like low-hanging fruit, waiting to be taken on board and used. The low-hanging fruit for Western Europe and Japan after WWII was the technology that had been invented in the US in the 1920s, 1930s, and 1940s. This is represented by I^* in Eqs. (1.1), (1.2), and (1.3). But to learn from others, a country needs some level of education and expertise so that people in business will both have the judgment to decide which foreign technologies and business ideas to take on board and the ability to understand and adapt to local circumstances. Robert Aliber, of Chicago Booth School of Business, often paraphrases a quote that is (mistakenly) attributed to Andy Warhol—that every country has its 30 years of growth—which is a restatement of the Nelson-Phelps model. But the statement needs to be qualified with the caveat that not every country can have its 30 years of growth, only those that have institutions such as an education system, the rule of law to some minimum degree, free trade, and functioning capital markets, to name some of the most essential preconditions.

But why, then, did the US, which is the technology leader in so many industries, slow down after 1973 or so? One explanation is diminishing

[3]The region with the highest social capital is Copenhagen in Denmark, followed by two smaller regions in Denmark and two regions in Sweden. The regions with the lowest social capital are in Slovenia, Poland, Bulgaria, and Romania. The countries with the values most conducive to labor market performance in Europe are the Nordic countries, the Netherlands, and Switzerland, followed by the UK, Germany, Ireland, and Austria. The Central European countries lag behind, as does Southern Europe. The countries of Eastern Europe come out last.

returns to I in the function $G\left(I_t, I_t^*, \zeta\right)$ in Eq. (1.2). The economic historian Joel Mokyr of Northwestern University has made the distinction between macroinventions and microinventions. Some examples of macroinventions are the internal combustion engine and the spinning wheel and in recent times artificial intelligence. Macroinventions have a big impact by creating whole new industries but only become effective through a series of microinventions, which are the small, incremental steps that improve and adapt existing techniques already in use. Microinventions are subject to diminishing returns, which would explain why the Second Industrial Revolution petered out in the second half of the twentieth century, as is described by Robert Gordon (2016).

There is a complementary explanation provided both in *Mass Flourishing* and in *Dynamism*. The message in those books is that there has been a fall in indigenous innovation in the West in recent decades. This can be attributed to a changing *Zeitgeist*, which has altered the values of the population. There is more emphasis on "to be" than "to do;" that is, people have a sense of entitlement based on who they are and what their profession is. There is a faint resemblance to attitudes in the 1920s, when many became attracted to corporatism. At that time, farmers and artisans and other interest groups sought protection, scientists and artists wanted state support, and religious groups sought the restoration of traditional communities. Today, there appears to be great dissatisfaction among many participants in the economies of the West. A lower rate of productivity growth is partly to blame, but also, according to this thesis, the lower rate of indigenous innovation in the workplace makes it less stimulating. But what could possibly explain the changing values in the US and the other Western countries?

There are signs of suffering among the workforce, which, in stark contrast to previous generations, no longer expects a rapidly growing standard of living. Angus Deaton found problems affecting the noncollege white population in the US. There is declining life expectancy due to suicide, opioid addiction, depression, and obesity. We argue in *Dynamism* that all this may be due to a loss of the values that fueled dynamism in the preceding decades and centuries. There is the change in the nature of jobs, as well as the loss of the experience of succeeding at something, both of which may drain much of the meaningfulness of many people's work.

President Carter's now infamous "malaise speech" in July 1979 provides a good description of the problems. At the root, said Carter, is a loss of faith in and the loss of the old values of hard work, strong families, closely knit communities, and faith in God. Instead, too many people tend to worship self-indulgence and consumption. For too many people, identity is no longer defined by what one does but by what one owns. They have discovered that only consuming things does not satisfy their longing for meaning. There is growing disrespect for government. Carter called for the restoration of American values as the alternative. Now, more than 40 years later, the US faces fragmentation, polarization, and the populism that came to the fore with the presidency of Donald Trump.

The West faces division and discontent, which takes many forms. There is widespread frustration over the lack of economic growth. Over the years there has been too little income growth, increased wealth and income inequality, and stagnant real wages. This is not caused by a loss of scientific discoveries but by a loss of innovation in our workplaces and in the creation of new firms. This slowdown has caused a decrease in the real rate of interest and in investment. The discontent is also caused by a fall in the relative wages of middle-income earners in many Western economies, those working in farming and manufacturing and those stranded in rural areas. Educated workers in cities have managed to raise their incomes by learning about new technologies, while rural people have not had the opportunity to do so. This failure to keep up has created disillusionment in rural areas among the noncollege educated, not just in the US but also in European countries.

Disadvantaged workers also suffer directly from some of the impediments to innovation. They may feel excluded and unable to move to the more innovative and dynamic urban economies, both because low house prices deter their mobility and because corruption, barriers to competition, cronyism, and other obstacles hinder them from having a shot at joining the well-educated urban population. The rise of identity politics has further alienated these people.

In this book, we turn our back on the modeling of uncertainty and the origins of job satisfaction. Instead, we take the fall in productivity growth as a given and describe the macroeconomic consequences for the real rate of interest, for stock prices, and for markups of price over marginal costs. We then turn to explaining the implications of the slowdown for the superpower rivalry between the US and China before describing policies that could help spur innovation and make the world a more contented and peaceful place.

References

Arnorsson, A., & Zoega, G. (2016). Social capital and the labor market. *Capitalism & Society, 11*(1), 1–29.

Bhidé, A. (2010). *The venturesome economy: How innovation sustains prosperity in a more connected world*. Princeton, NJ: Princeton University Press.

Gordon, R. J. (2016). *The rise and fall of American growth*. Princeton, NJ: Princeton University Press.

Nelson, R. R., & Phelps, E. S. (1966). Investment in humans, technological diffusion, and economic growth. *American Economic Review, 56*(1/2), 69–75.

CHAPTER 2

The Slowdown and Real Interest Rates

The COVID-19 crisis has hit the Western world at a time of weakness. In the past 40 years, productivity growth rates have fallen, public debt has increased in many countries, and real interest rates have fallen drastically. Keynesian orthodoxy has called for measures to stimulate aggregate demand, arguing that demand is deficient for a host of reasons. In this chapter, we argue that the problem is to be found on the supply side of the economy, in the slowdown of productivity growth that occurred in the 1970s when the rapid productivity growth in Europe, Japan, and the US in the 1950s and 1960s came to a screeching halt. The average rate of total factor productivity (TFP) growth in the G7 countries declined from decade to decade from the 1950s onward: from 3.62% in the 1950s to 1.96% in the 1970s, 1.17% in the 1990s, and 0.36% in the 2010s.[1]

2.1 One-Sector Neoclassical Model

We argue that low interest rates reflect a problem of low productivity growth. Supply-side factors explain the confluence of weak productivity growth, low real rates of interest, and stagnant real wages, as well as falling employment and labor force participation.

[1] Source: Bergeaud et al. (2022).

E. Phelps et al., *The Great Economic Slowdown*,
https://doi.org/10.1007/978-3-031-31441-4_2

We model the determination of the equilibrium real rate of interest in a one-sector neoclassical model in which the equilibrium occurs where the demand for capital equals the supply of wealth—or, alternatively, where saving equals investment, as in Wicksell (1898). The demand for capital derives from firms' profit maximization, while the supply of wealth comes from the maximization of lifetime utility by finitely-lived consumers. We assume that consumers have finite lifetimes, as in Blanchard (1985), a constant probability of death θ, and positive population growth n, as in Buiter (1988) and Weil (1989). Many people are born at each point in time, and θ is both the probability of death per unit time and the fraction of the total population that dies at each instant. Each agent derives utility from consumption, which we assume to be additively separable and taking the logarithmic form. Each consumer enters into a contractual agreement with an insurance company to receive a rate of return on their total financial assets at each instant while alive, in exchange for their entire estate upon death. Under the assumption of free entry and zero profit in the insurance industry, the insurance premium is θ per unit time.

Consumers have a subjective rate of time preference ρ and face a real rate of interest r. In steady state, we have consumption per capita growing at the rate of labor-augmenting productivity growth λ. We set the rate of growth of per capita consumption C in the Blanchard-Buiter-Weil model equal to λ and adopt the Euler equation for per capita consumption growth along the optimal path,

$$\lambda = r - \rho - (n+\theta)(\rho+\theta)\left[\frac{W}{C}\right], \tag{2.1}$$

where W is per capita nonhuman wealth. Using the consumption function $C = (\theta+\rho)(W+H)$ in Eq. (2.1), where H is per capita human wealth, gives

$$\lambda = r - \rho - (n+\theta)(\rho+\theta)\left[\frac{W}{(\theta+\rho)(W+H)}\right]. \tag{2.2}$$

Consumers receive a constant stream of income in the form of an annuity payment from perfectly competitive insurance companies, θW, in exchange for receipt of their wealth when they die. We define $y^W \equiv (r - \lambda + \theta) W$, where y^W is nonwage income, which grows at rate λ, as in Hoon and

Phelps (1997). This is growth-adjusted income from wealth. Canceling terms in the last term in Eq. (2.2) and noting that $H = \left(v\bar{L}\right)/\left(r-\lambda+\theta\right)$ in steady state, where v is the real wage and $\bar{L}$ is time endowment, gives

$$\lambda = r - \rho - \left[\frac{n+\theta}{1+\frac{v\bar{L}}{\left(r-\lambda+\theta\right)W}}\right]. \tag{2.3}$$

Inserting the expression for y^W into Eq. (2.3) and rearranging, we obtain

$$\lambda = r - \rho - \left[\frac{n+\theta}{1+\frac{v\bar{L}}{y^W}}\right]. \tag{2.4}$$

Rewriting Eq. (2.4), we have

$$r = \lambda + \rho + \left[\frac{n+\theta}{1+\frac{v\bar{L}}{y^W}}\right], \tag{2.5}$$

which makes the real interest rate r an increasing function of the rate of labor-augmenting productivity growth and a decreasing function of the wage-to-nonwage income ratio $\left(v\bar{L}/y^W\right)$. We can also express Eq. (2.3) as

$$W = \left[\frac{r-\lambda-\rho}{\left(n+\theta+\rho+\lambda-r\right)\left(r-\lambda+\theta\right)}\right]v\bar{L}. \tag{2.6}$$

Intuitively, higher real interest rates cause reduced consumption and increased saving through an intertemporal substitution effect, which gives an upward-sloping curve in the real wage–wealth space. This effect is strengthened by higher real rates lowering the level of human wealth, which reduces consumption further.

On the production side of the model, output is determined by an aggregative production function. The production function is assumed to be invariant over time. Let the production function be given by $Y = F(K, \Lambda N\bar{L})$, where K is the physical capital stock, $\Lambda_t = \Lambda_0 \exp(\lambda t)$ is the index of labor-augmenting technical progress, and $N_t = N_0 \exp(nt)$ is the size of the population (equal to the size of the labor force); furthermore, we assume for now that each worker works a fixed number of hours $\bar{L}$. It is twice differentiable with positive and diminishing marginal products. It satisfies the Inada conditions so that, taking limits, both the marginal product of labor and the marginal product of capital start at infinity and diminish to zero. Expressed in intensive form, we write $\tilde{y} = Y/(\Lambda N\bar{L}) = f(\tilde{k})$, where $\tilde{k} \equiv K/(\Lambda N\bar{L})$, and $f(\tilde{k})$ is a strictly concave monotonically increasing function. Perfect competition in goods and factor markets yields

$$r = f'(\tilde{k}) - \delta \text{ and} \tag{2.7}$$

$$\tilde{v} = f(\tilde{k}) - \tilde{k}f'(\tilde{k}), \tag{2.8}$$

where $\tilde{v} \equiv v/\Lambda$ and δ is the rate of physical capital depreciation.

Equations (2.7) and (2.8) together give the factor-price frontier

$$\tilde{v} = \phi(r); \phi'(r) < 0. \tag{2.9}$$

Using Eq. (2.9) in Eq. (2.6), we obtain

$$\frac{W}{\Lambda} = \left[\frac{r - \lambda - \rho}{(n + \theta + \rho + \lambda - r)(r - \lambda + \theta)}\right]\phi(r)\bar{L}. \tag{2.10}$$

A higher real rate of interest increases the supply of wealth through the intertemporal substitution effect and the human wealth effect as described previously. But there is a third effect working through the real wage. A higher real rate of interest lowers the level of capital $\tilde{k}$ as shown in Eq. (2.7), which then lowers the marginal product of labor and the real wage, as is shown in Eq. (2.8). In Eq. (2.10), this is captured by the factor-price frontier $\phi(r)$. We can describe these effects further by taking the derivative of the normalized nonhuman wealth W/Λ with respect to the real interest rate r, holding the real wage v constant:

$$\frac{d\left(\frac{W}{\Lambda}\right)}{dr}=\left[\frac{(n+\theta)(\theta+\rho)+(r-\lambda-\rho)^2}{(n+\theta+\rho+\lambda-r)^2(r-\lambda+\theta)^2}\right]\frac{v\bar{L}}{\Lambda}>0. \tag{2.11}$$

For given v/Λ, it follows that $d\left(\frac{W}{\Lambda}\right)/dr$ is positive. However, through the factor-price frontier, $v/\Lambda = \phi(r)$, $\phi'(r) < 0$, so an increase in r reduces the normalized real wage. The weight attached to the influence of $\phi(r)$ on the supply of wealth is given by $\left[\frac{r-\lambda-\rho}{(n+\theta+\rho+\lambda-r)(r-\lambda+\theta)}\right]$, which is increasing in r. Hence the supply-of-wealth curve can be backward-bending when r is high and the weight attached to the influence of the real interest rate on the real wage through the factor-price frontier is greater.

As regards demand for capital, by inverting Eq. (2.7) we obtain

$$\tilde{k}=\mu(r);\mu'(r)<0. \tag{2.12}$$

Since $\tilde{k}\equiv K/(\Lambda N\bar{L})$, it follows that

$$\frac{(K/N)}{\Lambda}=\mu(r)\bar{L}. \tag{2.13}$$

Equation (2.13) gives a downward-sloping demand-for-capital schedule. Demand for capital is decreasing in the real rate of interest and increasing in the time endowment $\bar{L}$. In the absence of public debt, Eqs. (2.10) and (2.13) give the supply-of-capital and demand-for-capital curves, respectively, as is shown in Fig. 2.1.

2.2 Productivity Growth Shock

A decrease in λ shifts the W/Λ schedule to the right, which we can show by taking the derivative of Eq. (2.10) with respect to λ:

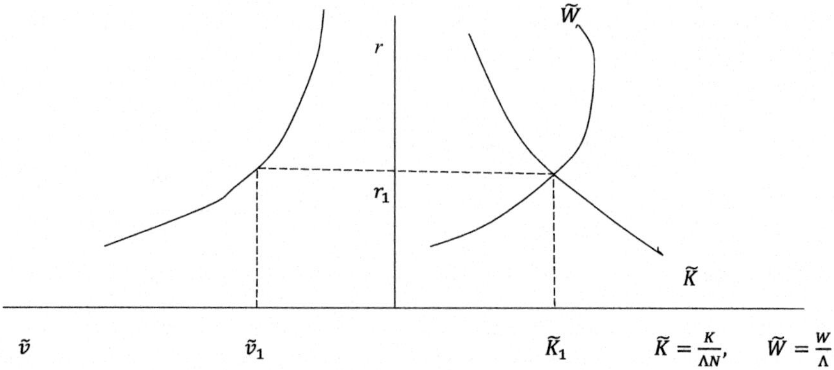

Fig. 2.1 Equilibrium in the capital market

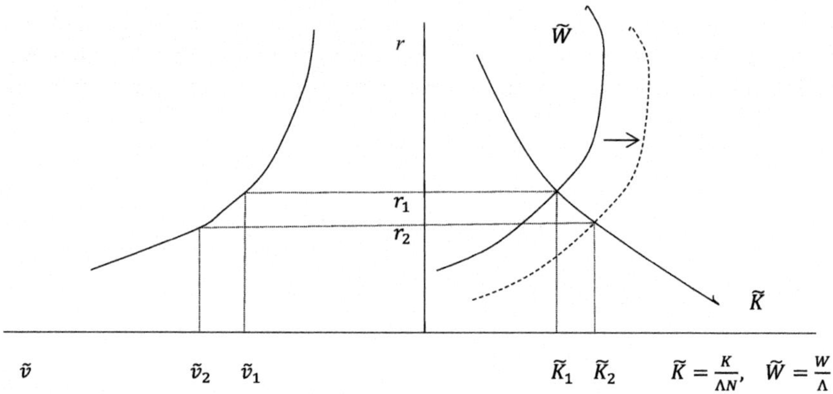

Fig. 2.2 The effect of a fall in the rate of productivity growth λ

$$\frac{d\left(\frac{W}{\Lambda}\right)}{d\lambda} = -\left[\frac{(n+\theta)(\theta+\rho)+(r-\lambda-\rho)^2}{(n+\theta+\rho+\lambda-r)^2(r-\lambda+\theta)^2}\right]\phi(r)\bar{L} < 0. \tag{2.14}$$

Because of the downward slope of the demand-for-capital schedule, the rate of interest falls and normalized wealth W/Λ is increased (see Fig. 2.2). Intuitively, the fall of λ makes the present discounted value of future wages fall; that is, human wealth H falls, which makes individuals save more.

However, in the new equilibrium, the rate of growth of both the real wage v and per capita nonhuman wealth W is reduced to the lower level of λ, noting that $\tilde{v} \equiv v / \Lambda$, so that the consumer is worse off.

The fall in the real rate of interest r that follows from the fall in the rate of productivity growth λ depends on the elasticities of the demand-for-capital and supply-of-wealth curves. For a given rightward shift of the supply-of-wealth curve, the smaller the sum of the two elasticities is, the greater the decline in the real rate of interest will be. If we let ϵ be the elasticity of the supply-of-wealth curve and η be the elasticity of the demand-for-capital curve, we have the following:

$$\frac{d\log(r)}{d\lambda} = \frac{-\left(d\log(W/\lambda)/d\lambda\right)}{\varepsilon + \eta} > 0, \tag{2.15}$$

by setting the supply-of-wealth curve equal to the demand-for-capital curve and taking the total derivative with respect to λ.

2.3 Decline in Population Growth

A decline in output growth can be caused by both a decline in productivity growth λ and a decline in the rate of population growth, n. Using Eq. (2.10), we can show that the effect of the latter is qualitatively similar to that of the former: both shift the supply-of-wealth curve to the right as in Fig. 2.2 causing the real rate of interest to fall. Taking the derivative of Eq. (2.10) gives

$$\frac{d\left(\frac{W}{\Lambda}\right)}{dn} = -\left[\frac{r - \lambda - \rho}{(n + \theta + \rho + \lambda - r)^2 (r - \lambda + \theta)}\right] \phi(r) \bar{L} < 0. \tag{2.16}$$

Since the derivate is negative, a fall in n makes the supply-of-wealth curve shift to the right.

Intuitively, a rise in n makes per capita aggregate consumption grow more slowly because of slower growth in nonhuman wealth, as newborns have no nonhuman wealth. Starting with growth of wages and consumption equal to λ, only a higher saving rate can restore the growth of wealth and consumption to an unchanged level of λ.

2.4 Helicopter Drop of Public Debt

We now add government debt to the model. An increase in the level of public debt will create a new form of wealth due to consumers' finite horizons and the entry of new disconnected families into the economy:

$$\frac{W}{\Lambda} = \frac{(K/N)}{\Lambda} + \tilde{D},$$

where $\tilde{D} \equiv D/\Lambda$ is the per capita stock of public debt normalized by the index of labor-augmenting technical progress. As individuals are not linked through intergenerational transfers—that is, bequests—to all those born after them, the resources of future generations are not included in their intertemporal budget constraints. Consequently, the issuance of public debt is nonneutral. The effect of an increase in the stock of public debt in the form of a helicopter drop is then to create a wedge between nonhuman wealth and the capital stock (appropriately normalized), as is shown in Fig. 2.3. The effect is to reduce the stock of (normalized) capital and increase the real rate of interest.

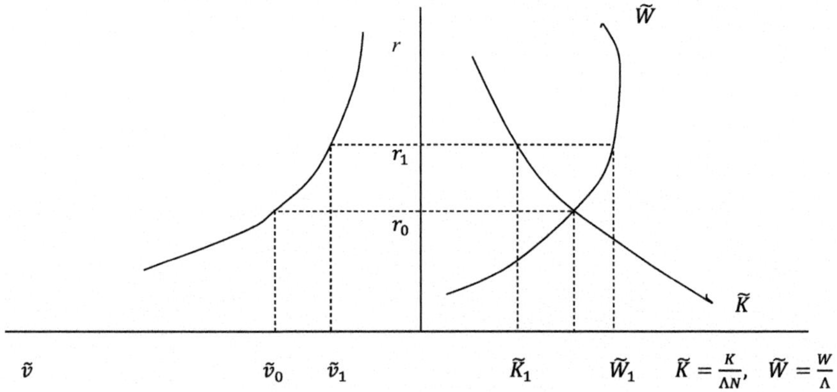

Fig. 2.3 The effect of a helicopter drop of public debt

The percentage increase of the real interest rate in response to a percentage increase in the stock of (normalized) public debt is given by

$$\frac{d\log(r)}{d\log(\tilde{D})} = \frac{\tilde{D}/(W/\Lambda)}{\varepsilon + [(K/N\Lambda)/(W/\Lambda)]\eta}, \tag{2.17}$$

where η is the elasticity of the demand-for-capital curve and ϵ is the elasticity of the supply-of-wealth curve. We saw that a decline in λ leads to a large drop in the real interest rate if ε and η are small. Here an increase in public debt leads to a large increase in the real rate if ε and η are small. But we see that it is not simply the sum, $\epsilon + \eta$, that matters for the response of the real interest rate to an increase in the stock of public debt. Rather, the initial size of the stock of public debt relative to total nonhuman wealth also matters, the effect going through both the numerator and the denominator of the right-hand side of Eq. (2.17). Because the size of the public debt rises as a share of total nonhuman wealth, each percentage increase in the stock of public debt has a larger proportionate impact on the real interest rate.

We have mentioned previously that, according to Blanchard (2019), fiscal deficits may have limited fiscal costs due to low interest rates. Also, according to Furman and Summers (2020), in a world of cheap capital, concerns about crowding out of private investment are not important. Thus Blanchard, Furman, and Summers argue that the reduction of the capital stock does not affect output much if the real rate of interest is close to zero. However, in the present model we find that increased public debt may increase interest rates if the demand-for-capital schedule is steep and the interest rate effect grows stronger as the share of public debt in total nonhuman wealth grows larger. Thus, currently low interest rates per se do not provide sufficient grounds for the claim that concerns about the crowding out of capital are not important.

We have found that a fall in the rate of productivity growth and an increase in the stock of public debt have opposite effects on the real rate of interest and the normalized stock of capital. A fall in the rate of productivity growth will lower the real rate of interest, but an increase of the stock of public debt will raise it. Moreover, the responsiveness of the real interest rate to the rise in the stock of public debt increases as public debt becomes a larger share of total nonhuman wealth.

2.5 The Stock of Housing

Suppose that the felicity function at a given point in time of an individual is the sum of the log of consumption of a nondurable good and the log of housing services, which is taken to be proportional to the per capita stock of housing. In the model of Sect. 2.1 we then add the condition

$$\frac{C}{S} = r + \delta, \tag{2.18}$$

where C is per capita consumption of the nondurable goods and S is the per capita stock of housing. The equation sets the marginal rate of substitution between nondurable and durable consumption equal to the rental price of housing $r + \delta$. A lower rental price makes consumers consume relatively more housing services. Thus, relative to the consumption of the nondurable good, there is an increase in the housing stock if the decline in the rate of Harrod-neutral technical progress causes a decline in the real interest rate, as derived in Sect. 2.2 of this chapter.

We have shown that a decline in λ results in an increase in W/Λ and $(K/N)/\Lambda$. We now wish to show that a decline in λ causes both $(K/N)/\Lambda$ and (S/Λ) to increase, as it leads to a decline in the real rate of interest. To see this, we use $C = (\theta + \rho)[W + H]$ in Eq. (2.18) to obtain

$$\frac{(\theta + \rho)[W + H]}{S} = r + \delta. \tag{2.19}$$

Noting that $W = (K/N) + S$ in the absence of public debt, we obtain

$$(\theta + \rho)\left[1 + \frac{(K/N)/\Lambda}{S/\Lambda} + \frac{\tilde{v}\bar{L}}{(r - \lambda + \theta)(S/\Lambda)}\right] = r + \delta, \tag{2.20}$$

where $\tilde{v}$ is normalized wages. Using Eqs. (2.9) and (2.12) in Eq. (2.20), we have

$$(\theta + \rho)\left[1 + \frac{\mu(r)\bar{L}}{S/\Lambda} + \frac{\phi(r)\bar{L}}{(r - \lambda + \theta)(S/\Lambda)}\right] = r + \delta. \tag{2.21}$$

We note from Eq. (2.12) that, given the real interest rate, demand for productive capital $(K/N)/\Lambda$ by firms is independent of the housing stock (S/Λ). Firms choose to build their factories without consideration of the housing stock for a real interest rate. Equation (2.20) set the marginal rate of substitution between nondurable consumption and housing services equal to the rental on capital. It follows from the equation that given the real interest rate, consumer demand for the housing stock depends directly on the stock of productive capital. Intuitively, holding the rental and the rate of depreciation constant, a larger stock of capital means more wealth because households own the capital stock, which then gives more consumption, making them want to increase their housing stock.

From Eq. (2.21) the dependence of demand for housing on the real interest rate, after considering the dependence of the productive capital stock on the real interest rate, is given by

$$\frac{d(S/\Lambda)}{dr}=\frac{-\left[\frac{1}{\theta+\rho}+\frac{\phi(r)\bar{L}}{(r-\lambda+\theta)^2(S/\Lambda)}-\frac{\phi(r)\bar{L}}{(r-\lambda+\theta)(S/\Lambda)}-\frac{\mu'(r)\bar{L}}{S/\Lambda}\right]}{\frac{\mu(r)\bar{L}}{(S/\Lambda)^2}+\frac{\phi(r)\bar{L}}{(r-\lambda+\theta)(S/\Lambda)^2}}<0. \tag{2.22}$$

Using Eq. (2.22), total demand for housing and the physical capital stock (appropriately normalized) curve is given by $\frac{S}{\Lambda}+\frac{\frac{K}{N}}{\Lambda}\equiv\frac{S}{\Lambda}+\tilde{k}\bar{L}$, where $\tilde{k}\equiv\frac{K}{\Lambda N\bar{L}}=\mu(r)$, with a negative slope given by

$$\frac{d(S/\Lambda)}{dr}+\mu'(r)\bar{L}<0,$$

where the first term is given by Eq. (2.22). It follows that higher real interest rates make demand for housing fall when considering the effect on demand for capital. Intuitively, higher interest rates r make firms demand less capital, which lowers the stock of nonhuman wealth held by consumers, who then reduce their consumption of both nondurable consumption and housing services.

The supply-of-wealth curve is, in turn, given by Eq. (2.10). A decline in the rate of Harrod-neutral technical progress results in a rightward, and hence downward, shift of the supply-of-wealth curve as in the model

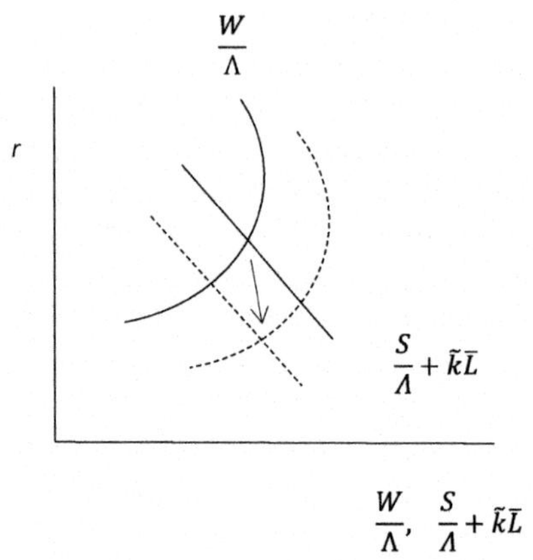

Fig. 2.4 Effects of a decline in λ in a model with housing wealth

without housing, when households expect slower future wage growth and increase saving as a result. The decline in the rate of technological progress also shifts total demand for housing and the physical capital stock leftward, and hence also downward, for the same reason. Intuitively, weaker expected wage growth makes human wealth fall, which then makes consumers reduce both nondurable consumption and demand for housing services. This additional shift in demand for the two types of assets, housing and capital stock, causes a further decline in the real interest rate (Fig. 2.4).

Intuitively, the decline in λ lowers the future rate of growth of wages, making human wealth drop instantaneously, which then makes consumption fall, as well as demand for housing. The fall in demand for housing makes the rental on capital fall, which then makes demand for productive capital $\tilde{k}$ increase.

2.6 Endogenous Labor Force Participation

So far, we have assumed that the labor force participation rate and employment are constant. [2] In this section, we relax this assumption and explore the effects of the technology slowdown on employment.

[2] Phelps (1999) explained the US employment boom of the late 1990s in terms of stronger productivity growth, and Phelps and Zoega (2001) showed how the long swings in employment in the OECD countries from 1960 onwards could be explained by changes in the stock market, which proxied for the shadow price of capital, customers, and trained labor. Fitoussi and Phelps (1988) argued that the fiscal and monetary shocks originating in the USA in the early 1980s played a causal role in the rise of unemployment in Europe.

With constant probability of death, we face the possibility that some individuals will live forever (in our theoretical model) and will have a rising consumption profile over their lifetimes, even when the economy is in a steady state. While all individuals, independent of age, have the same wage rate per unit of time worked, they differ in their level of wealth depending on age. The older the individual, the more wealth he will have. These old individuals may want to retire from the workforce because they want to increase leisure as well as consumption in proportion to their increasing wealth. To preserve tractability in aggregating across individuals, Hoon (2011) develops a theoretical economy in which every individual alive has an incentive to spend a positive (though variable) number of hours in the market sector, depending on their wage-to-nonhuman wealth ratio.

We can write the labor force participation rate $L/\bar{L}$ as a positive function of the wage-to-non-wage income ratio. We start with an equation that equates the marginal rate of substitution between consumption and leisure to the real wage:

$$\frac{\bar{L}-L}{C}=\frac{A+1}{v}, \tag{2.23}$$

where utility is the sum of the log of consumption of each consumer and the sum of the utility of his leisure, and A+1 is a positive multiplicative factor in front of the log of leisure in the utility function, measuring the value of leisure. We can then use the Blanchard-Buiter-Weil consumption function $C = (\theta + \rho)(W + H)$ and the value of human wealth $H = vL/(r - \lambda + \theta)$ in steady state. Defining $y^W \equiv (r - \lambda + \theta)W$, we obtain an expression for labor supply:

$$\frac{L}{\bar{L}}=\frac{1-(A+1)\left[\dfrac{\theta+\rho}{r-\lambda+\theta}\right]\left(\dfrac{v\bar{L}}{y^W}\right)^{-1}}{1+(A+1)\left[\dfrac{\theta+\rho}{r-\lambda+\theta}\right]}. \tag{2.24}$$

The labor supply curve is increasing in the ratio of the "full wage" $v\bar{L}$ to nonwage income ratio and represented by the upward-sloping curve in Fig. 2.5. When $v\bar{L}$ goes up relative to nonwage income y^W, individuals work more because the opportunity cost of leisure is now higher. A high

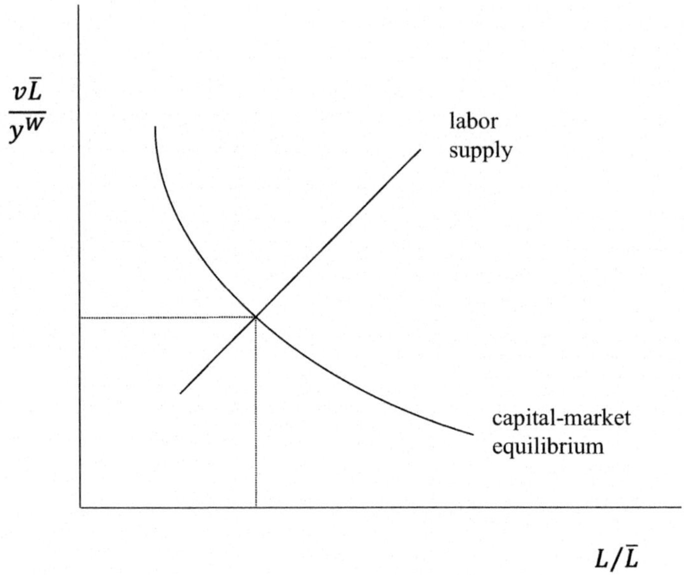

Fig. 2.5 Equilibrium with endogenous labor supply

value of nonwage income y^W relative to potential wage income $v\bar{L}$ will make workers work fewer hours, reducing $L/\bar{L}$. Moreover, an increase in the real rate of interest will increase labor supply $L/\bar{L}$ when workers have an interest in working more to earn a higher income, which they can invest at a higher real rate of interest.

For the downward-sloping relationship in the figure, we start again with the Blanchard-Buiter-Weil Euler equation, Eq. (2.1), using the consumption function and the equation for human wealth as previously defined to obtain

$$r - \lambda = \rho + \frac{n+\theta}{1+\left(\frac{v\bar{L}}{y^W}\right)\left(\frac{L}{\bar{L}}\right)}. \tag{2.25}$$

The Blanchard-Buiter-Weil relationship gives the optimal path of consumption and saving in the model, and due to Eq. (2.23), which gives the optimal ratio of consumption, it also gives the optimal path of leisure. For a given value of real interest rates, the equation gives a downward-sloping relationship between the wage-to-nonwage income ratio and labor L. We refer to this downward-sloping relationship as *capital market equilibrium*. Starting in equilibrium, if v were to increase, raising $v\bar{L}/y^W$, consumption would increase for a given required real rate of interest. The effect is to lower the required real rate of interest for the capital market equilibrium to hold. For a given real rate of interest, employment $L/\bar{L}$ must fall when real wages $v\bar{L}/y^W$ rise.

Our model consists of a labor supply relationship, a capital market equilibrium condition, and, by Walras' law, a goods market equilibrium. The first two solve for two endogenous variables, $L/\bar{L}$, and $v\bar{L}/y^W$, where $\bar{L}$ and y^W are exogenous variables.

We have shown that labor supply is upward sloping in $v\bar{L}/y^W$. Turning to capital market equilibrium, since the product $\left(\frac{v\bar{L}}{y^W}\right)\left(\frac{L}{\bar{L}}\right)$ must remain constant over time for a given r, we obtain a downward-sloping hyperbolic relationship between $\left(\frac{v\bar{L}}{y^W}\right)$ and $\left(\frac{L}{\bar{L}}\right)$, shown in Fig. 2.5.

Along an optimal path where both Eqs. (2.24) and (2.25) hold, real wages v and consumption are rising if $\lambda > 0$, but leisure remains unchanged because the opportunity cost of leisure, which is the real wage, is rising over time, offsetting the greater demand for leisure caused by rising consumption. Also, since v is growing at rate λ along the optimal consumption path, nonwage income y^W must also rise at the same rate. In other words, since H is rising at rate λ, nonhuman wealth and hence y^W must increase at the same rate so that consumption C can rise at that rate.

From Eq. (2.24), given $v\bar{L}/y^W$, an increase in r - λ raises $L/\bar{L}$ by lowering the value of human capital H. When people are poorer because of a lower expected rate of growth of wages, they respond by reducing both consumption and leisure, shifting the upward-sloping labor supply curve to the right. However, using Eq. (2.25), an increase in r - λ also reduces $\left(\frac{vL}{y^W}\right)$, through a fall in either v or L (Fig. 2.6). This makes the hyperbolic downward-sloping relationship shift downward toward the origin. If we assume that this second channel dominates, then we have

$$\frac{L}{\bar{L}} = \Phi(r-\lambda); \Phi'(r-\lambda) < 0.$$

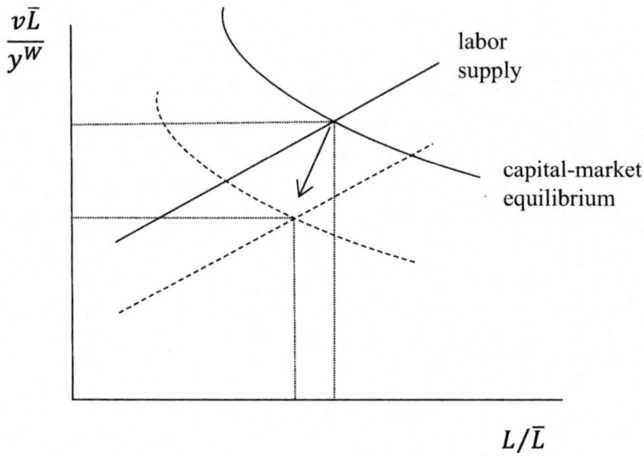

Fig. 2.6 The effect of an increase in $(r - \lambda)$

Intuitively, we can think of the downward shift of the labor supply curve as being caused by a higher $r - \lambda$ reducing human capital, which lowers both consumption and leisure. What remains to explain is the downward shift of the downward-sloping hyperbolic relationship–the capital market equilibrium. In essence, an increase in $r - \lambda$ requires nonhuman wealth W to increase relative to consumption along the optimal path, which requires human wealth to fall, occurring through either lower wages v or reduced L. In other words, an increase in the required real rate of interest calls for a fall in the wage-to-non-nonwage income ratio so that consumption will be lower for a given level of nonhuman wealth. The movement down the new labor supply curve represents workers reducing their labor supply as their wage falls relative to their nonwage income.

We have taken $r - \lambda$ as given. We now turn to making the real interest rate endogenous to our model. From Eqs. (2.5) and (2.24), and noting that $y^W \equiv (r - \lambda + \theta)W$, we obtain a per capita supply of nonhuman wealth:

$$W = \left[\frac{(r-\lambda-\rho)(L/\bar{L})}{(n+\theta+\rho+\lambda-r)(r-\lambda+\theta)}\right] v\bar{L}, \tag{2.26}$$

where L and $\bar{L}$ appear separately in the equation, in contrast to Eq. (2.10). Because $L/\bar{L} = \Phi(r-\lambda)$, we then have

$$\frac{W}{\Lambda} = \left[\frac{(r-\lambda-\rho)\Phi(r-\lambda)}{(n+\theta+\rho+\lambda-r)(r-\lambda+\theta)}\right]\phi(r)\bar{L}, \tag{2.27}$$

where $v/\Lambda = \phi(r)$ is the factor-price frontier.

There is also the demand-for-capital schedule. In place of Eq. (2.13), we have the following schedule

$$\frac{(K/N)}{\Lambda} = \mu(r)\Phi(r-\lambda)\bar{L}, \tag{2.28}$$

which comes from inverting $r = f'(\tilde{k}) - \delta$, where N is the number of workers, in contrast to L, which is the time spent working by each worker.

Now we come to the effect of a decrease in λ on labor force participation $L/\bar{L}$, when r is determined in full general equilibrium. We show that $r - \lambda$ may rise, which would lead to a decrease in the labor force participation rate, $L/\bar{L}$, as we have just shown.

The fall in participation changes our earlier analysis of the effect of a fall in λ on the equilibrium real rate of interest with a fixed and exogenous labor supply. There (see Fig. 2.2) the fall in λ lowers the future expected growth of wages, which makes human capital drop, consumption fall, and the supply of saving increase, lowering the real rate of interest. Now, the lower participation rate L leads to a decrease in demand for capital since each worker spends fewer hours working the machines, shifting the $(K/N)/\Lambda$ curve in Fig. 2.7—which corresponds to our earlier Fig. 2.2—to the left. Working fewer hours makes capital less productive, so that demand for it declines. We saw earlier that, in the case of a fixed labor force participation rate, a decrease in λ leads to a rightward shift of the supply-of-wealth curve in Fig. 2.2 when households respond to a fall in their human capital by lowering consumption. With the labor force participation rate endogenous, the decrease in $L/\bar{L}$ at a given r attenuates the downward shift of the supply-of-wealth curve because people save less when they work less. Overall, if r falls by less than λ does, then a productivity growth slowdown leads to a fall in the labor force participation rate and the real interest rate.

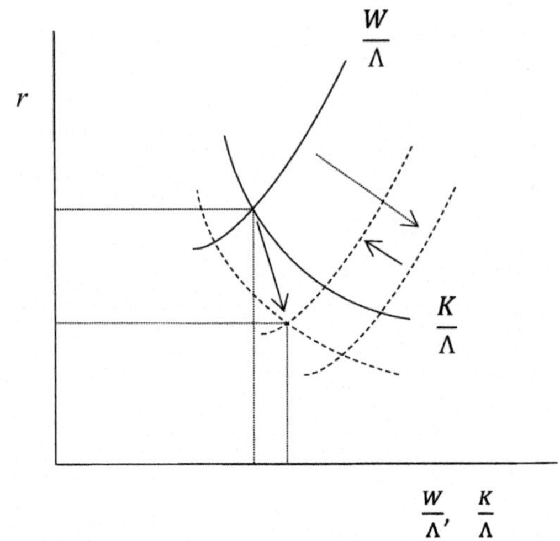

Fig. 2.7 The effect of a decline in λ if r - λ is increased

In Fig. 2.7, the supply-of-wealth curve shifts less to the right than before, and the demand-for-capital schedule shifts downwards. The net effect on r- λ is positive as the figure shows, while r falls unambiguously. Hence a decline in λ may cause r - λ to increase, so that if r falls, it falls by less than λ does, and labor participation falls as well.[3]

We now turn to the effect of changes in job satisfaction in the model. A decrease in the level of job satisfaction—captured by a rise in A in Eq. (2.23), which is the value attached to labor increases or disutility of labor—has the effect of shifting the upward-sloping labor supply curve to the left.

In the book *Mass Flourishing* by Phelps, a fall in the rate of innovation λ lowers job satisfaction, i.e., increases the disutility of labor A. As can be seen in Fig. 2.5, the effect would be to shift the upward-sloping supply-of-labor curve to the left, raising the ratio of the real wage to nonwage income and reducing the supply of labor by each working individual. The rise in the ratio of the real wage to nonwage income is due to a fall in nonwage income because the real wage is fixed for a given real rate of interest. The fall in y^w is caused by workers' lower wage income, vL, reducing their saving and hence their income from their stock of savings.

[3] It is possible that r - λ falls when λ falls, in which case labor supply would increase, making the rightward shift of the supply-of-wealth curve greater and making the demand-for-capital curve shift rightwards.

References

Bergeaud, A., Cette, G., & Lecat, R. (2022, November 24). *The long-term productivity database*. Prod. Bank of France.http://www.longtermproductivity.com/about.html.

Blanchard, O. (1985). Debt, deficits, and finite horizons. *Journal of Political Economy, 93*(2), 223–247.

Blanchard, O. (2019). Public debt and low interest rates. *American Economic Review, 109*(4), 197–229.

Buiter, W. H. (1988). Death, birth, productivity growth and debt neutrality. *Economic Journal, 98*(391), 279–293.

Fitoussi, J.-P. & Phelps, E. S. (1988). *The Slump in Europe*. Oxford: Blackwell.

Furman, J., & Summers, L. (2020). *A reconsideration of fiscal policy in the era of low interest rates*. Brookings Institution. furman-summers-fiscal-reconsideration-discussion-draft.pdf.

Hoon, H. T. (2011). Payroll taxes, wealth, and employment in neoclassical theory: Neutrality or nonneutrality. In Edmund S. Phelps & Hans-Werner Sinn (Eds.), *Perspectives on the performance of the Continental economies* (pp. 429–445). Cambridge, MA: MIT Press.

Hoon, H. T., & Phelps, E. S. (1997). Growth, wealth and the natural rate: Is Europe's jobs crisis a growth crisis? *European Economic Review, 41*(3-5), 549–557.

Phelps, E. S. (1999). Behind this structural boom: The role of asset valuations. *American Economic Review: Papers and Proceedings, 89*(2), 63–68.

Phelps, E. S., & Zoega, G. (2001). Structural Booms. *Economic Policy, 16*(32), 84–126.

Weil, P. (1989). Overlapping families of infinitely-lived agents. *Journal of Public Economics, 38*(2), 183–198.

Wicksell, K. (1898). *Interest and prices*. Macmillan & Co.

CHAPTER 3

The Slowdown and Asset Prices

One of the stylized facts of economic development in recent decades, reviewed in the introductory chapter, is the booming stock market. In this chapter we derive the implications of the slowdown in growth for asset prices. We model the effect of a decline in productivity growth on the real interest rate, capital, wealth, and asset prices. For this, we use what may be called an "Austrian model," where capital is produced only with labor in the investment-good sector and the consumer good is produced using only capital in the consumer-goods sector. The price of capital in terms of the consumer good is the asset price in the model. We first derive the model in steady state and generate the demand-for-capital schedule as well as the supply-of-wealth schedule when agents have finite horizons and there is entry into the economy of new families that are unconnected to each other. We then provide a dynamic analysis of the economy's response to an unanticipated decrease in the rate of Harrod-neutral technical progress. It is shown that asset prices rise in response to such a shock.

3.1 A Two-Sector Austrian Model

Basic Setup

As in the last chapter, we assume that consumers have finite lifetimes as in Blanchard (1985), a constant probability of death θ, and positive population growth through the entry of unconnected families into the economy

E. Phelps et al., *The Great Economic Slowdown*, https://doi.org/10.1007/978-3-031-31441-4_3

as in Buiter (1988) and Weil (1989). Each agent derives utility from consumption, which we assume to be additively separable and to take the logarithmic form. Consumers have a rate of time preference ρ and face a real rate of interest r. The production functions for the consumer good and the investment good are

$$Z_C = \Pi_K K,\ Z_I = \Lambda N\bar{L},$$

where N is the number of workers hired and each worker supplies $\bar{L}$ number of hours.

Using the definition of nonhuman wealth gives (see derivation in Chap. 1)

$$W = \left[\frac{r-\lambda-\rho}{(n+\theta+\rho+\lambda-r)(r-\lambda+\theta)}\right] v\bar{L}, \tag{3.1}$$

which is Eq. (2.6) in Chap. 2. To relate the real wage v to the real interest rate, we note that if the output of the investment good depends only on augmented labor and if the output of the consumer good per unit of capital is given by Π_K, then profit maximization of price-taking firms gives

$$(r+\delta)q_k = \Pi_K \tag{3.2}$$

for the use of capital in the production of the consumer good, where the rental on capital is equal to the marginal product of capital measured in units of the consumer good. Alternatively, the rate of return on capital Π_K/q_k net of depreciation is equal to the real rate of interest. In the investment-good sector, labor is hired until the value of the marginal product of labor Λq_k is equal to the real wage v, which, after rearranging, gives Eq. (3.3):

$$\tilde{v} = q_k, \tag{3.3}$$

where $\tilde{v} \equiv v/\Lambda$, δ is the rate of physical capital depreciation, and q_k is the shadow price of a unit of physical capital. Equation (3.2) tells us that the shadow price of a unit of physical capital is equal to the present discounted value of the stream of marginal product of capital, taking into account physical capital depreciation. Equation (3.3) tells us that the real wage normalized by the index of Harrod-neutral technical progress is given by the shadow price of physical capital. Substituting for q_k in Eq. (3.3) using Eq. (3.2), we obtain

$$\tilde{v} = \frac{\Pi_K}{r+\delta}, \tag{3.4}$$

which gives the factor-price frontier. Then, substituting for v in Eq. (3.1) using Eq. (3.4) gives the supply-of-wealth schedule:

$$\frac{W}{\Lambda} = \left[\frac{r-\lambda-\rho}{(n+\theta+\rho+\lambda-r)(r-\lambda+\theta)}\right]\left(\frac{\Pi_K}{r+\delta}\right)\bar{L}. \tag{3.5}$$

This relationship is represented by the upward-sloping curve in the right-hand quadrant of Fig. 3.1, showing a positive relationship between real interest rates and normalized wealth.

To derive the demand-for-capital schedule $q_k K/(N\Lambda)$, which is the value of capital per efficiency unit of labor, we note that, in steady state,

$$\Lambda N\bar{L} = (n+\lambda+\delta)K,$$

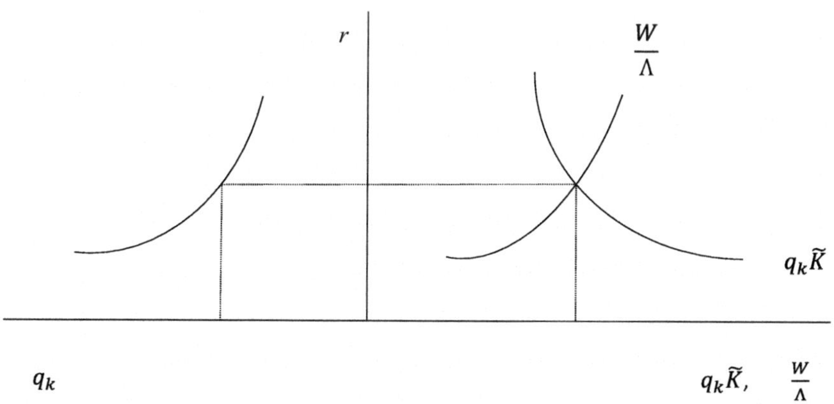

Fig. 3.1 Determination of real interest rates

so that the production of the investment good, the left-hand side of the equation, is equal to required investment for the capital stock to grow at rate λ. The equation can be rewritten as follows,

$$\tilde{K} \equiv \frac{K}{N\Lambda} = \frac{\bar{L}}{n+\lambda+\delta}, \tag{3.6}$$

where we define $\tilde{K} \equiv K/(N\Lambda)$ as the normalized stock of capital per unit of effective labor. Equation (3.6) sets the actual level of investment equal to the level required in steady state. Using Eq. (3.2) in Eq. (3.6) and multiplying both sides by q_k, the demand-for-capital schedule is given by

$$q_k\tilde{K} = \left[\frac{\bar{L}}{n+\lambda+\delta}\right]\left(\frac{\Pi_K}{r+\delta}\right). \tag{3.7}$$

The demand-for-capital schedule is shown as the downward-sloping curve in the right-hand quadrant of Fig. 3.1, showing a negative relationship between real interest rates and the demand for capital when each unit of capital is valued by q_k. As r decreases, each unit of capital is valued more highly.

The left-hand quadrant has a relationship that relates the real interest rate to the asset price using the factor-price frontier and Eq. (3.3).

What is the effect of a decrease in λ on the real interest rate? At given r, the decrease in λ shifts the supply-of-wealth schedule to the right, as in Chap. 2, but it also shifts the demand-for-capital schedule to the right, so it appears that the effect on r is ambiguous. The reason the demand-for-capital schedule shifts to the right is that the decline in λ leads to capital deepening; that is, an increase in $\tilde{K}$. The shift of the supply curve shows the effect of increased saving due to a fall in expected future wage growth. Thus, a fall in λ involves a rightward shift in both the downward-sloping curve and the upward-sloping curve. In fact, we can show that the effect of a decrease in λ is to cause the real interest rate to fall.

To see why real interest rates fall, we set the rate of growth of per capita consumption in the Blanchard-Buiter-Weil model equal to λ and adopt the Euler equation for consumption growth along the optimal path:

$$\lambda = r - \rho - (n+\theta)(\rho+\theta)\left[\frac{W}{C}\right], \tag{3.8}$$

where W is per capita nonhuman wealth. Noting that $W = q_k K/N$ and $C = \Pi_K K/N$, we obtain

$$\lambda = r - \rho - (n+\theta)(\rho+\theta)\left[\frac{q_k}{\Pi_K}\right]. \tag{3.9}$$

Using Eq. (3.2) in Eq. (3.9) and rearranging, we obtain

$$r = \lambda + \rho + (n+\theta)(\rho+\theta)\left[\frac{1}{r+\delta}\right]. \tag{3.10}$$

Differentiating r with respect to λ in Eq. (3.10), we obtain

$$\frac{dr}{d\lambda} = \frac{1}{1+\frac{(n+\theta)(\rho+\theta)}{(r+\delta)^2}} > 0,$$

which tells us that a decline in λ must unambiguously lower the real rate of interest. We note from the left-hand quadrant of Fig. 3.2 that as the real

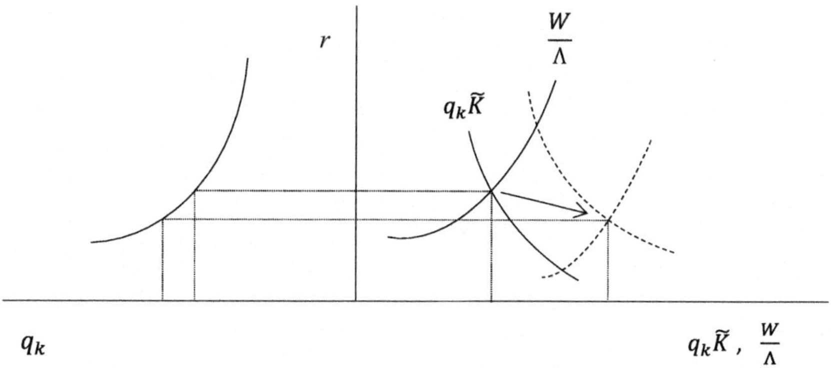

Fig. 3.2 Effect of a fall in productivity growth

interest rate declines, the shadow price of a unit of physical capital increases. While this has the effect of raising the normalized real wage, the real wage now grows at a slower rate given by the lower rate of productivity growth.

A fall in population growth n will have a similar effect on the real interest rate and the shadow value of capital. A fall in n makes the supply-of-wealth curve shift to the right. The logic behind the shift is the same as in Chap. 2. A decline of n makes per capita aggregate consumption grow faster because of more rapid growth in nonhuman wealth, since newborns have no nonhuman wealth. Starting with growth of wages and consumption equal to λ, only a higher saving rate can restore the growth of wealth and consumption to an unchanged level of λ.

The demand-for-capital schedule also shifts to the right because the decline in n leads to capital deepening; that is, an increase in $\tilde{K}$. The net effect is to unambiguously make the real rate of interest fall because the shift of the supply-of-wealth schedule is greater than the shift of the demand-for-capital schedule, as can be seen by taking the total differential of Eq. (3.10) to obtain

$$\frac{dr}{dn} = \frac{\dfrac{\rho+\theta}{r+\delta}}{1+\dfrac{(n+\theta)(\rho+\theta)}{(r+\delta)^2}} > 0. \tag{3.11}$$

We can sum up the discussion by saying that both a fall in the rate of productivity growth λ and a fall in the rate of population growth n have the effect of lowering the real rate of interest and raising the shadow price of capital. In both cases, there is an instantaneous increase in the real wage, but the slope of the future path differs depending on whether there is a fall in λ or a fall in n. In the former case, weaker productivity growth makes real wages grow at a slower rate in the future, while weaker population growth has no effect on the slope of the future path of real wages.

A one-off increase in Π_K increases demand for capital at a given real rate of interest as shown in Eq. (3.7) by making capital more productive in the production of the consumer good. From Eq. (3.5), we can also see that the supply of wealth increases for a given interest rate. The intuition for the increased supply of wealth comes from the Stolper-Samuelson theorem. An increase in Π_K by raising the demand for capital makes the price of the investment good q_k increase, which causes the payment to labor

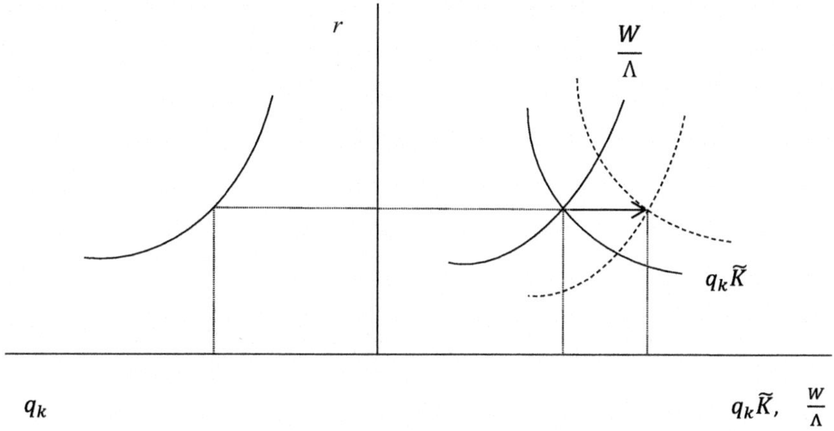

Fig. 3.3 Increase in the productivity of capital in the consumer-goods sector

(used intensively in the production of the investment good) to rise. The net effect is to increase the stock of wealth and capital but to leave the real rate of interest unchanged, as is shown in Fig. 3.3.

Dynamics

We now turn to dynamics and examine the dynamic response of the economy to an unanticipated decline in productivity growth. The two key dynamic equations that determine the general-equilibrium behavior of the economy described in terms of q_k and $\tilde{K} \equiv K/(N\Lambda)$ given an initial $\tilde{K}_0$ are

$$\dot{\tilde{K}} = \bar{L} - (n + \lambda + \delta)\tilde{K}; \tag{3.12}$$

$$\dot{q}_k = \left\{ \rho + (n+\theta)(\rho+\theta)\left(\frac{q_k}{\Pi_K}\right) + \frac{\bar{L}}{\tilde{K}} - n \right\} q_k - \Pi_K. \tag{3.13}$$

Equation (3.13) comes from noting that the required interest rate from capital market equilibrium is given by

$$r = \left\{ \rho + (n+\theta)(\rho+\theta)\left(\frac{q_k K}{\Pi_K K} \right) \right\} + \frac{\dot{C}}{C}.$$

Since the consumer goods market must clear so that NC = $\Pi_K K$, it follows that

$$\frac{\dot{C}}{C} = \frac{\dot{K}}{K} - n.$$

We can then take logs of $\tilde{K} \equiv K/(N\Lambda)$, and then it follows that

$$\frac{\dot{K}}{K} = \frac{\dot{\tilde{K}}}{\tilde{K}} + n + \lambda.$$

Using Eq. (3.12), we can write

$$\frac{\dot{K}}{K} - n = \frac{\bar{L}}{\tilde{K}} - \delta - n.$$

It follows that

$$r = \left\{ \rho + (n+\theta)(\rho+\theta)\left(\frac{q_k K}{\Pi_K K} \right) \right\} + \frac{\bar{L}}{\tilde{K}} - \delta - n.$$

Observing that there is an asset pricing relationship, we write

$$r = \frac{\Pi_K}{q_k} + \frac{\dot{q}_k}{q_k} - \delta.$$

Equating the last two equations gives Eq. (3.13). For $\dot{q}_k = 0$, we obtain

$$\frac{\Pi_K}{q_k} = \left\{ \rho + (n+\theta)(\rho+\theta)\left(\frac{q_k}{\Pi_K} \right) + \frac{\bar{L}}{\tilde{K}} - n \right\}. \tag{3.13'}$$

Equation (3.12) tells us how capital per augmented worker evolves over time, the steady state being shown in Equation (3.6). Equation (3.13) comes from first noting that $C = \Pi_K K/N$. Taking the log on both sides and then taking the time derivative, the rate of growth of per capita consumption is equal to the rate of growth of capital per worker. There is an arbitrage between the total yield from holding physical capital as an asset and the instantaneous real rate of interest, which we may call the asset pricing relationship. Using the Euler equation giving the growth rate of per capita consumption in the Blanchard-Buiter-Weil model, as well as Eq. (3.12) in the asset pricing relationship, we obtain Eq. (3.13). The steady state solution is shown in Eq. (3.13').

The stationary $\tilde{K}$ locus is a vertical line at $\tilde{K}_{ss} = \bar{L}/(n+\lambda+\delta)$, while the stationary q_k locus is positively sloped in the ($\tilde{K}$, q_k) plane. The system exhibits saddle-path stability. The saddle path shows that the shadow value of a unit of physical capital is an increasing function of capital per effective worker. If the capital stock per effective worker is, say, below its steady-state level so that it is rising toward that level, the shadow value of a unit of physical capital will likewise be rising (Fig. 3.4).

A decline in λ shifts the stationary $\tilde{K}$ locus to the right because the investment required to maintain the steady-state level falls. There is an immediate upward jump of q_k, and the economy traverses along an upward-sloping path to reach a new steady state with higher $\tilde{K}$ and q_k. Intuitively, the real interest rate declines instantaneously, making q_k jump, and as the real rate of interest declines further on the path to the new steady state, the value of q_k gradually converges to its higher steady-state value (Fig. 3.5).

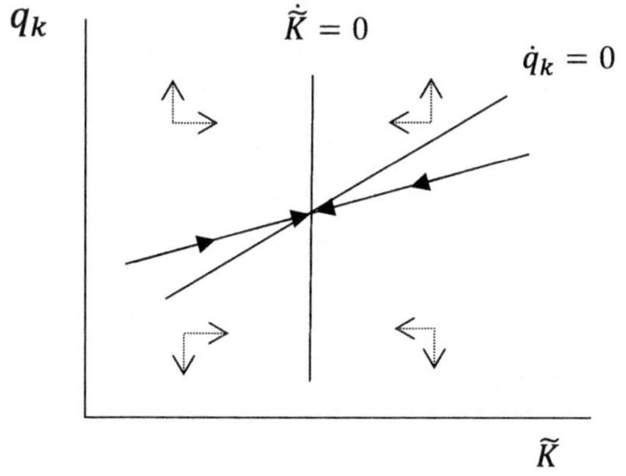

Fig. 3.4 Saddle-path stability

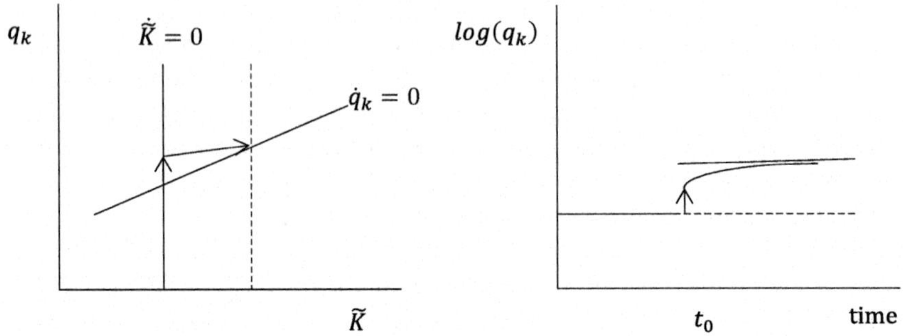

Fig. 3.5 Sudden unanticipated drop in λ

We now introduce public debt $\hat{D} \equiv D/(\Pi_K K)$, which will appear in Eq. (3.13), so that rewriting (3.13') gives

$$\frac{\Pi_K}{q_k} = \left\{ \rho + (n+\theta)(\rho+\theta)\left(\frac{q_k}{\Pi_K} + \hat{D}\right) + \frac{\bar{L}}{\tilde{K}} - n \right\}. \qquad (3.13'')$$

A helicopter drop of debt $\hat{D}$ drives up the real rate of interest in the Buiter-Weil framework, which makes the $\dot{q}_k = 0$ locus shift downwards, making q_k drop instantaneously. The downward shift is further explained in the lower half of Fig. 3.6, where the right-hand-side of Eq. (3.13") shifts upwards.

Labor-Leisure Choice

We now change our model by making labor supply endogenous. We use the utility function $u(C_i, L_i) = \log(C_i) + (A+1)\log(\bar{L} - L_i)$ for individual i with $A > 0$. Allowing individuals to adjust the number of hours they work, the per capita labor supply is given by

$$L = \bar{L} - \frac{(A+1)C}{\nu}. \qquad (3.14)$$

In the absence of public debt, per capita consumption C satisfies the Euler equation

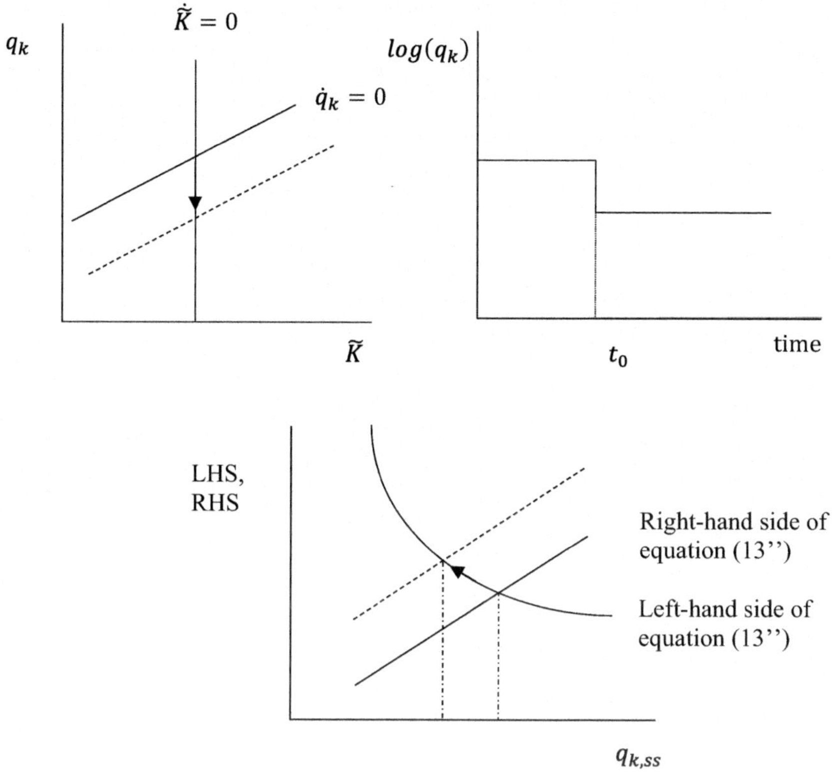

Fig. 3.6 Helicopter drop of public debt

$$\frac{\dot{C}}{C} = r - \rho - (n + \theta)(\rho + \theta)\left(\frac{q_k K}{\Pi_K K}\right). \tag{3.15}$$

In the spirit of the Austrian perspective of capital theory, only labor is required to produce the investment good, and only physical capital is required to produce the consumption good. Hence, $Z_I = \Lambda NL$ and $Z_C = \Pi_K K$. The capital accumulation equation is given by

$$\dot{K} = \Lambda NL - \delta K. \tag{3.16}$$

Clearing of the consumer-goods market requires

$$\mathrm{NC} = \Pi_K K, \tag{3.17}$$

and profit maximization of price-taking firms in the investment-good sector gives

$$\frac{v}{\Lambda} = q_k. \tag{3.18}$$

Using Eqs. (3.17) and (3.18) in Eq. (3.14), we have

$$L = \bar{L} - \frac{(A+1)\Pi_K K}{\Lambda N q_k}. \tag{3.19}$$

Defining $\tilde{K} \equiv K/(N\Lambda)$, we can rewrite Eq. (3.16) as

$$\frac{\dot{\tilde{K}}}{\tilde{K}} = \frac{\bar{L}}{\tilde{K}} - \frac{(A+1)\Pi_K}{q_k} - (n+\lambda+\delta), \tag{3.20}$$

using Eq. (3.19), which then becomes

$$L = \bar{L} - \frac{(A+1)\Pi_K \tilde{K}}{q_k}. \tag{3.21}$$

Using Eq. (3.17) in Eq. (3.15), we obtain an expression for the instantaneous real interest rate

$$\begin{aligned} r &= \rho + (n+\theta)(\rho+\theta)\left(\frac{q_k}{\Pi_K}\right) + \frac{\dot{K}}{K} - n \\ &= \rho + (n+\theta)(\rho+\theta)\left(\frac{q_k}{\Pi_K}\right) + \frac{\dot{\tilde{K}}}{\tilde{K}} + \lambda \end{aligned} \tag{3.22}$$

by subtracting and adding λ to the first line of the equation. Using Eq. (3.20) in Eq. (3.22), we obtain

$$r = \rho + (n+\theta)(+\theta)\left(\frac{q_k}{\Pi_K}\right) + \frac{\bar{L}}{\tilde{K}} - \frac{(A+1)\Pi_K}{q_k} - n - \delta. \tag{3.23}$$

Equation (3.23) gives the required real rate of interest. The asset pricing equation is given by

$$r = \frac{\Pi_K}{q_k} - \delta + \frac{\dot{q}_k}{q_k}, \tag{3.24}$$

which gives the real rate of return on capital. Together, using Eq. (3.23) in Eq. (3.24), we obtain the dynamic equation giving the rate of growth of q_k

$$\frac{\dot{q}_k}{q_k} = \rho + (n+\theta)(\rho+\theta)\left(\frac{q_k}{\Pi_K}\right) + \frac{\bar{L}}{\tilde{K}} - \frac{(A+2)\Pi_K}{q_k} - n. \tag{3.25}$$

A decline in λ leads to an immediate upward jump in q_k, followed by a rising path of q_k, as is shown in Fig. 3.7. The effect of this change on labor supply can be seen from Eq. (3.21). If, along the rising path in Fig. 3.7, $q_k / \tilde{K}$ declines—the slope of the saddle path is less than one—then per capita labor supply, after an initial upward jump, declines to reach a permanently lower labor supply if the final steady state $q_{k,ss} / \tilde{K}_{ss}$ is lower at the new steady state—which again follows from the slope of the saddle path being less than one.

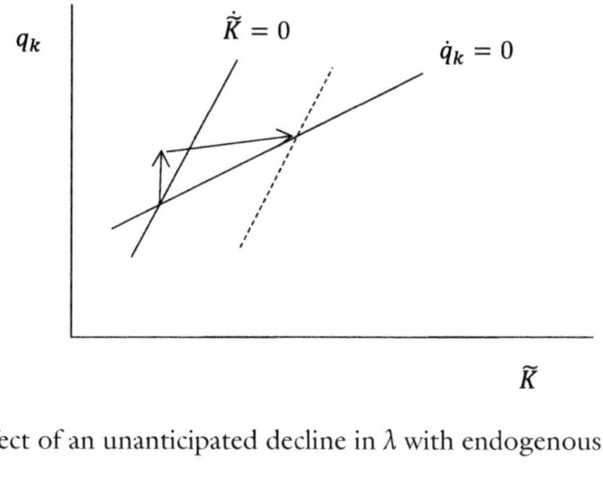

Fig. 3.7 Effect of an unanticipated decline in λ with endogenous labor supply

Substitution between Labor and Capital

The Austrian model where labor is used only in the production of the investment good while the production of the consumer good uses only physical capital gives rise to a transformation curve relating the two outputs that is rectangular. We can modify the model to allow substitution possibilities along the transformation curve. We assume that while only labor is required in the production of the investment good, both physical capital and labor are necessary in the production of the consumer good. Hence, $Z_I = \Lambda N_I \bar{L}$ and $Z_C = F\left(K, \Lambda N_C \bar{L}\right) = \Lambda \bar{L} N_C f\left(k_C\right)$, where $k_C \equiv K / \left(\Lambda N_C \bar{L}\right)$. Labor is allocated across the two sectors so that

$$N = N_I + N_{C.} \tag{3.26}$$

Dividing both sides of Eq. (3.26) by N, we have

$$1 = n_I + n_C; n_I \equiv \frac{N_I}{N}; n_C \equiv \frac{N_C}{N}. \tag{3.27}$$

Defining $\tilde{k} \equiv K / \left(\Lambda N \bar{L}\right)$, we can write, using Eq. (3.27),

$$\tilde{k} = \frac{k_C}{\left(\frac{n_I}{1 - n_I}\right) + 1}. \tag{3.28}$$

We also note that

$$\frac{Z_C}{\Lambda N \bar{L}} = \frac{\tilde{k} f\left(k_C\right)}{k_C}; \frac{d\left(\frac{f\left(k_C\right)}{k_C}\right)}{dk_C} < 0; \tag{3.29}$$

$$\frac{Z_I}{\Lambda N \bar{L}} = \frac{n_I}{\tilde{k}} = \frac{1}{\tilde{k}} - \frac{1}{k_C}. \tag{3.30}$$

The capital accumulation equation is given by

$$\dot{K} = \Lambda N_I \bar{L} - \delta K, \tag{3.31}$$

which we can re-express as

$$\frac{\dot{\tilde{k}}}{\tilde{k}} = \frac{1}{\tilde{k}} - \frac{1}{k_C} - (n + \lambda + \delta). \tag{3.32}$$

Profit maximization by price-taking firms in both the investment good and consumer good sectors gives

$$\tilde{v} = q_k = f(k_C) - k_C f'(k_C), \tag{3.33}$$

$$R = f'(k_C) \tag{3.34}$$

where $\tilde{v} \equiv v/\Lambda$ and R is the capital rental. From Eq. (3.33), we have that k_C is uniquely pinned down by q_k (as long as labor is used in both sectors) and is positively related to q_k:

$$\frac{dk_C}{dq_k} = \frac{-1}{k_C f''(k_C)} > 0. \tag{3.35}$$

The asset pricing relationship is given by

$$r = \frac{R}{q_k} - \delta + \frac{\dot{q}_k}{q_k},$$

which, using Eq. (3.34), can be expressed as

$$r = \frac{f'(k_C)}{q_k} - \delta + \frac{\dot{q}_k}{q_k}. \tag{3.36}$$

The consumer's Euler equation can be written as

$$\frac{\dot{C}}{C} = r - \rho - (n + \theta)(\rho + \theta)\left(\frac{q_k K}{NC}\right),$$

which, after setting $C = Z_C/N$ and using Eq. (3.29), can be further re-expressed as

$$\frac{\dot{C}}{C} = r - \rho - (n+\theta)(\rho+\theta)\left(\frac{q_k k_C}{f(k_C)}\right). \tag{3.37}$$

Writing

$$\frac{f(k_C)}{k_C} = \omega(k_C); \omega'(k_C) < 0$$

and expressing the condition that the market for the consumer good clears as $C = \Lambda \bar{L} \tilde{k} \omega(k_C)$, we obtain

$$\frac{\dot{C}}{C} = \lambda + \frac{\dot{\tilde{k}}}{\tilde{k}} + \left[\left(\frac{q_k \omega'(k_C)}{\omega(k_C)}\right)\left(\frac{dk_C}{dq_k}\right)\right]\frac{\dot{q}_k}{q_k}. \tag{3.38}$$

Using Eq. (3.32) in Eq. (3.38), we obtain

$$\frac{\dot{C}}{C} = \frac{1}{\tilde{k}} - \frac{1}{k_C} - (n+\lambda) + \left[\left(\frac{q_k \omega'(k_C)}{\omega(k_C)}\right)\left(\frac{dk_C}{dq_k}\right)\right]\frac{\dot{q}_k}{q_k}. \tag{3.39}$$

Using Eq. (3.39) in Eq. (3.37), we obtain the required rate of interest:

$$r = \rho + (n+\theta)(\rho+\theta)\left(\frac{q_k k_C}{f(k_C)}\right) + \frac{1}{\tilde{k}} - \frac{1}{k_C} - (n+\delta) + \left[\left(\frac{q_k \omega'(k_C)}{\omega(k_C)}\right)\left(\frac{dk_C}{dq_k}\right)\right]\frac{\dot{q}_k}{q_k}. \tag{3.40}$$

Equating Eq. (3.36) to Eq. (3.40), we obtain

$$\left\{1 - \left[\left(\frac{q_k \omega'(k_C)}{\omega(k_C)}\right)\left(\frac{dk_C}{dq_k}\right)\right]\right\}\frac{\dot{q}_k}{q_k} = \rho + (n+\theta)(\rho+\theta)\left(\frac{q_k k_C}{f(k_C)}\right) + \frac{1}{\tilde{k}} - \frac{1}{k_C} - n + \frac{f'(k_C)}{q_k}. \tag{3.41}$$

Equations (3.32) and (3.41) give the pair of dynamic equations, summarizing the general-equilibrium behavior of the economy given an initial value of $\tilde{k}$. We obtain saddle-path stability.

An unanticipated decline in λ causes an immediate upward jump in q_k followed by a steady rise of q_k along the transition to the new steady state with a higher q_k and $\tilde{k}$. Thus we find that generalizing the Austrian model by allowing for substitution possibilities along the transformation curve, which relates the output of the investment good and the output of the consumer good, does not change our key finding in this chapter: that a decline in the rate of growth of Harrod-neutral technical progress leads to a steady rise in the shadow value of a unit of physical capital.

A sudden helicopter drop of public debt does not shift the stationary capital per effective worker locus but shifts the stationary q_k locus downwards. The shadow value of a unit of physical capital immediately drops due to an increase in the real rate of interest, which lowers the present discounted value of future capital rentals and then continues to decline until it reaches a new steady state with decreased q_k and capital per effective worker (Fig. 3.8).

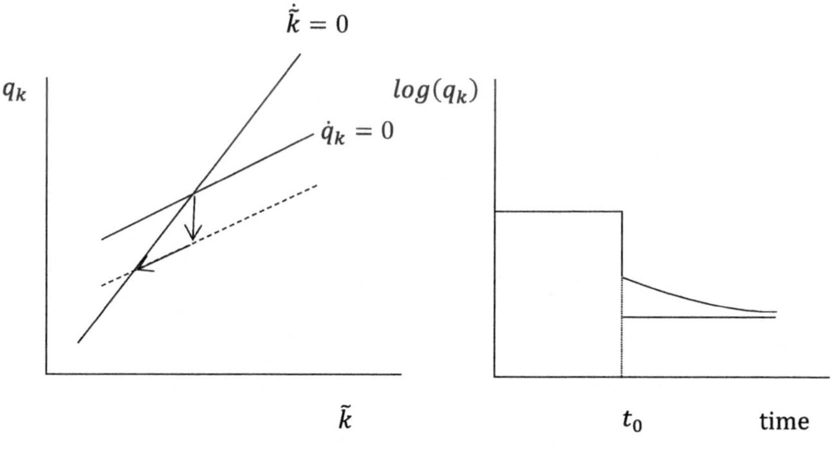

Fig. 3.8 Helicopter drop of public debt

3.2 Conclusions

In this chapter, we derived the implications of the slowdown in productivity growth for asset prices using what we call the "Austrian model," where capital is produced only with labor in the investment-good sector and the consumer good is produced using only capital. The price of capital in terms of the consumer good is the asset price in the model.

A fall in the rate of both productivity and population growth will lower the real rate of interest and raise the price of capital by increasing the supply of wealth. In contrast, an increase in government debt drives up the real rate of interest, making the price of capital drop.

References

Blanchard, O. (1985). Debt, deficits, and finite horizons. *Journal of Political Economy, 93*(2), 223–247.

Buiter, W. H. (1988). Death, birth, productivity growth and debt neutrality. *Economic Journal, 98*(391), 279–293.

Weil, P. (1989). Overlapping families of infinitely-lived agents. *Journal of Public Economics, 38*(2), 183–198.

CHAPTER 4

The Slowdown and the Share of Profits

In this chapter, we explain the rising share of profits in national income and the corresponding fall in the share of wages. De Loecker et al. (2020) have documented a significant rise in average markups in the US from 1955 onward. They find that average markups were 21% above marginal cost in 1980 but have risen to 61% by 2019. While median markups have not changed much, the upper percentiles have increased significantly. In addition, the market share of the high-markup firms has increased within industry.

To explain the rise in markups, we use the Phelps-Winter customer-market model of the product market to describe how markups are affected by the productivity growth slowdown. In contrast to Chap. 2, we take labor supply as given throughout the analysis. This chapter builds on the Austrian model in Chap. 2 by introducing the customer-market model in the consumer-goods sector. This leaves us with two assets: physical capital and customers.

A feature of the Phelps-Winter model is that the markup is a decreasing function of the shadow price of a customer taken as a ratio to current consumption per customer. When customers become more valuable—due to higher expected future demand and lower expected real rates of interest—relative to their current consumption, firms cut markups to expand their market share. In this way they invest in customers, and the return on the investment is the future profits from a larger market share. In a symmetric

E. Phelps et al., *The Great Economic Slowdown*,
https://doi.org/10.1007/978-3-031-31441-4_4

equilibrium, market shares are unchanged but markups are lower. In this chapter, we use this insight to describe the effect of a decline in the productivity growth rate on the shadow price of capital and customers and the markup of price over marginal cost. We show how weaker productivity growth leads to a rise in the shadow price of capital through a lower real rate of interest. The fall in the real interest rate makes steady-state consumption jump and the ratio of the shadow price of a customer relative to current consumption per customer drop. The result is higher markups. The increased current consumption raises the marginal cost of cutting markups, which dominates the positive effect of a higher shadow price of customers. Thus, a decline in the rate of productivity growth has the effect of both raising the value of capital and raising profits as a share of national income, which is consistent with the stylized facts of a booming stock market and a rising share of profits in national income observed in the US. We now turn to deriving the two-sector model with a customer market.

We start by laying out the basics of the Phelps-Winter customer-market model before introducing the transitional dynamics. Our departure from the original Phelps-Winter model is to introduce the two-sector Austrian model used in the previous chapter.

4.1 Basic Setup

There are two sectors in the economy: an investment-good sector and a consumer-goods sector. In the Phelps-Winter model, informational friction impedes a quick flow of customers to a firm that lowers its price below the price charged elsewhere in the economy. We make the simplifying assumption that informational frictions are only present in the market for consumer goods (with a customer base whose size is exogenously given by the population size). The investment-good market is perfectly competitive, while the consumer-goods market is described by the Phelps-Winter customer-market model. There are thus two assets in the economy: the stock of physical capital and the stock of customers. The production functions

$$Q_I = \Lambda N\overline{L}; \;\; Q_C = \Pi_K K$$

are linear, and we define the normalized capital stock as $\tilde{K} \equiv K/(\Lambda N)$, where N is the number of workers, each supplying $\overline{L}$ hours; Λ denotes the level of labor productivity, and the rate of growth of productivity is $\lambda = \dot{\Lambda} / \Lambda$.

Each firm in the consumption-good sector chooses the price at which to sell to its current customers. Lowering its price causes an increase in the quantity demanded by its current customers according to a per-customer demand relationship $\eta(p_i/p)$, which we assume is homogeneous of degree one in total sales: $\eta(1)C$ in a symmetric equilibrium. Note that $\eta'(1) < 0$. The rate of growth of the customer stock at a firm is a decreasing function of its price relative to the average price, with $g(1) = n$ and $g'(1) < 0$ in a symmetric equilibrium.

A firm in the consumer-goods sector chooses its relative price p_i/p to maximize the present discounted value of future profits from its customers, subject to the constraint

$$\dot{x} = g\left(\frac{p_i}{p}\right)x, g'(\bullet) < 0.$$

The decision involves a tradeoff between current and future profits. High markups increase current profits but at the cost of losing customers and future profits. At the optimum, these two effects are balanced at the margin. Letting m denote the gross markup of price over marginal cost, the markup is given by the following value-maximizing condition

$$1 + \frac{1}{\eta'(1)} - \frac{1}{m} = -\left(\frac{q_x}{C}\right)\left[\frac{g'(1)}{\eta'(1)}\right], \tag{4.1}$$

which makes the gross markup m negatively related to the shadow price of a customer q_x taken as a ratio to consumption per customer C denoted as $\hat{q}_x \equiv q_x / C$. The term on the right-hand side of the equation is negative because both $g'(1)$ and $\eta'(1)$ are negative. The term $1 + 1/\eta'(1)$ is marginal revenue, and the term $1/m$ is the marginal cost.

It follows that at optimum, the marginal revenue is lower than the marginal cost, and the producer produces more than the volume that maximizes monopoly profits. The consumer-goods firm lowers the price below the monopoly price to invest in a larger market share in the future. The level of this investment depends on the shadow price of customers relative to consumption per customer: $\hat{q}_x \equiv q_x / C$, the sensitivity of the customer base x to changes in relative prices, $g'(1)$, and the slope of the demand curve $\eta'(1)$. The greater the value of a customer and the easier it is to attract customers, the further prices are below their monopoly level.

In contrast, the higher current consumption is and the flatter the demand curve, the closer prices are to their monopoly level. The equation can also be written as

$$1+\frac{1}{\eta'(1)}+\left(\frac{q_x}{C}\right)\left[\frac{g'(1)}{\eta'(1)}\right]=\frac{1}{m},$$

where the left-hand side is the marginal benefit of cutting prices—both currently, through higher demand, and in the future, because of an expanded market share—and the right-hand side is the marginal cost of lowering prices. The higher the shadow price of customers is, the greater the marginal benefit from lowering prices and the lower the optimal price will be. It follows that $m=\Psi(\hat{q}_x);\Psi'(\hat{q}_x)<0$. In a symmetric equilibrium, all firms decide on the same markup; hence a single firm's attempt to invest in an expanded market share is met by price cuts from other firms, leaving market shares unchanged but prices lower.

Focusing on the steady state, where the production of the investment good $\Lambda N\bar{L}$ is equal to required investment $(n + \lambda + \delta)K$, we have

$$\tilde{K}=\frac{\bar{L}}{n+\lambda+\delta}. \tag{4.2}$$

We can characterize Eq. (4.2) as a vertical line in a back-to-back diagram with the value of capital q_k on the vertical axis and the normalized capital stock $\tilde{K}$ on the horizontal axis in the right-hand quadrant, and on the left-hand quadrant we have a relationship between q_k and the shadow price of a customer normalized by current consumption $\hat{q}_x$. See Fig. 4.1.

On the right-hand quadrant, we can also depict a relationship between q_k and the normalized capital stock arising from the following equation

$$r+\delta=\frac{\Pi_K}{q_k\Psi(\hat{q}_x)}, \tag{4.3}$$

where the markup is $m = \Psi(\hat{q}_x)$. This equation gives the shadow price of capital as the discounted stream of future marginal product of capital after taking into account the markup, which reduces the share of marginal product going to the owners of capital. We can also tie the equation to the golden rule of Phelps (1961) since it shows the relationship between the rental of capital $r + \delta$ and the rate of return on capital Π_K/q_k. The markup creates a divergence between the two, so that the higher the markup $\Psi(\hat{q}_x)$ is, the lower the real rate of interest for a given rate of return on capital will be. Therefore, a low real rate of interest does not have to imply dynamic inefficiency so that increased public debt may lower output and consumption even when real interest rates are close to zero. This relationship was implicit in Phelps and Winter (1970).[1]

Next we invoke the Blanchard-Buiter-Weil framework used in Chap. 2 to describe the behavior of finitely-lived consumers with $\dot{C}/C = \lambda$ in steady state and $\lambda = \frac{\bar{L}}{\tilde{K}} - n - \delta$ from Eq. (4.2). The latter can be rewritten as the equality of required investment and the production of the investment good, $(\lambda + n + \delta)K = \Lambda N\bar{L}$. It follows that

$$r = \rho + (n+\theta)(\rho+\theta)\left(\hat{q}_x + \frac{q_k}{\Pi_K}\right) + \frac{\bar{L}}{\tilde{K}} - n - \delta. \tag{4.4}$$

Using Eq. (4.4) in Eq. (4.3), we obtain Eq. (4.5), which is the asset-pricing relationship for capital:

$$\left\{\rho + (n+\theta)(\rho+\theta)\left(\hat{q}_x + \frac{q_k}{\Pi_K}\right) + \frac{\bar{L}}{\tilde{K}} - n\right\} q_k = \frac{\Pi_K}{\Psi(\hat{q}_x)}. \tag{4.5}$$

Note from the equation that all three endogenous variables of the system appear: $\hat{q}_x, q_k,$ and $\tilde{K}$. For a given $\hat{q}_x$, we have a positively sloped schedule relating q_k to $\tilde{K}$. The positive slope reflects the negative effect of

[1] See also Mankiw (2022) for a similar point. Mankiw (2022) uses the Solow growth model to derive the rental on capital as a function of the steady-state capital stock and the rate of depreciation, the former being a function of the saving rate and the rate of growth of the economy. He draws on Ball and Mankiw (2023) to show that rising market power can explain the fall in the real rate of interest for a given marginal product of capital.

higher $\tilde{K}$ on the rental of capital and the real rate of interest, which then raises q_k.

A decrease in $\hat{q}_x$ shifts the schedule to the right. The reason is that a lower $\hat{q}_x$ makes consumer-goods firms raise their markups, which decreases in steady state the returns on physical capital because the owner of the capital stock receives a smaller share of output. This effect would make the curve shift to the right; that is, it would lower the shadow price of capital q_k. But there is another offsetting effect where a lower $\hat{q}_x$ reduces wealth and therefore lowers the rate of interest, which then raises q_k and shifts the upward-sloping relationship to the left.

We next turn to deriving a negative relationship between q_k and the shadow price of a customer normalized by current consumption. The asset pricing relationship for customers is given by

$$r = \frac{1 - m^{-1}}{\hat{q}_x} + \lambda + n, \tag{4.6}$$

where the right-hand side is the rate of return on customers, which consists of the sum of the ratio of profits per customer to the shadow price of a customer and a capital gain term. The capital gain consists both of rising productivity, which makes customers' real wages and consumption grow, and of growth in the number of customers. Substituting for the gross markup m in Eq. (4.6) using Eq. (4.1), we obtain

$$(r - \lambda - n)\hat{q}_x = \frac{-1}{\eta'(1)} - \hat{q}_x \left[\frac{g'(1)}{\eta'(1)} \right]. \tag{4.7}$$

We can rewrite the equation as

$$\hat{q}_x = -\frac{\dfrac{1}{\eta'(1)} + \hat{q}_x \left[\dfrac{g'(1)}{\eta'(1)} \right]}{r - \lambda - n} = \frac{1 - \dfrac{1}{m}}{r - \lambda - n},$$

so that $\hat{q}_x \left(\equiv \frac{q_x}{C} \right)$ is again the present discounted value of future profits per consumption unit per customer. Using the equation above and the Blanchard-Buiter-Weil Euler equation,

$$r-\lambda=\rho+(n+\theta)(\rho+\theta)\left(\hat{q}_x+\frac{q_k}{\Pi_K}\right),$$

we obtain the following equation,

$$\left\{\rho+(n+\theta)(\rho+\theta)\left(\hat{q}_x+\frac{q_k}{\Pi_K}\right)+\left[\frac{g'(1)}{\eta'(1)}\right]-n\right\}\hat{q}_x=-\frac{1}{\eta'(1)}, \qquad (4.8)$$

which is a negative relationship between $\hat{q}_x$ and q_k. In effect, a higher q_k increases the real rate of interest through a wealth effect on consumption, which lowers the shadow price of customers, as is shown in Eq. (4.7). Going back to our diagram (Fig. 4.1), which has the price of capital q_k on the veritical axis and the shadow price of customers $\hat{q}_x$ on the left-hand side of the horizontal axis, from Eq. (4.8) we see that $\hat{q}_x$ is negatively related to q_k so that an increase in q_k must cause $\hat{q}_x$ to decrease.

4.2 Decline of Productivity Growth

We can now describe the effect of a decline in the rate of productivity growth λ on markups m and the shadow price of capital q_k. Here it matters that we are in a non-Ricardian world. A lower level of λ makes firms expect slower growth in consumption per customer. Workers expect a lower rate of growth of wages and increase the supply of saving, which lowers the equilibrium real rate of interest. The lower interest rate offsets the effect of lower λ on the value of a customer, but with finite lives, interest rates fall less than λ does because a higher value of capital raises consumption demand. It follows that $r - \lambda$ goes up, which lowers the value of a customer and causes firms to raise markups.

We can describe the effect of the fall in λ in more detail. The fall in λ causes the normalized capital stock to increase and the supply of saving to increase. The first effect shows up in the shift of the vertical capital supply curve to the right, while the negative effect of increased saving on real interest rates makes the shadow price of capital increase as we move along the upward-sloping asset price curve. The effect is then to lower the real rate of interest, which increases the shadow price of capital as we move up along the asset pricing schedule for capital in the right-hand quadrant of Fig. 4.1. While a lower real rate of interest increases q_x, the level of

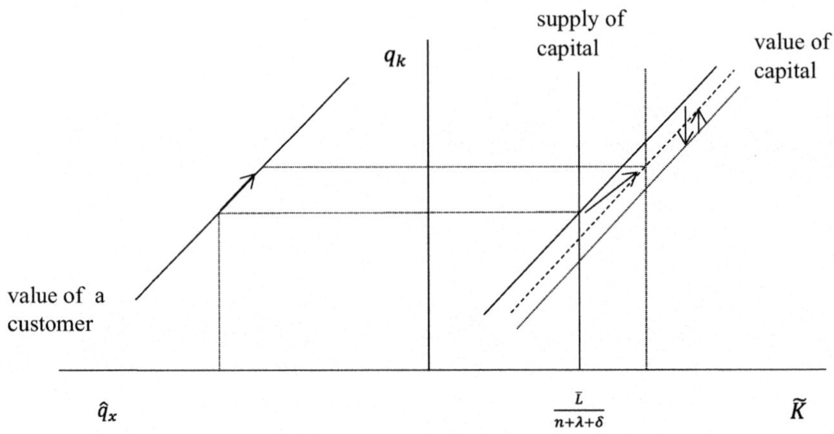

Fig. 4.1 The effect of a fall in productivity growth

consumption per customer C jumps due to the rise in q_k, which raises the stock of nonhuman wealth, making $\hat{q}_x \equiv q_x / C$ fall.

There are two other effects that work through the relationship between q_k and $\hat{q}_x$ in the left-hand quadrant. First, the fall in $\hat{q}_x$ has the effect of making markups m increase, which then reduces the rental income of households and the value of capital q_k—the upward-sloping curve in the right-hand quadrant of the figure shifts to the right and lowers the value of q_k. The second effect works in the other direction by shifting the curve to the left. The higher value of q_k increases household wealth and hence consumer demand through the Blanchard-Buiter-Weil equation, which has the effect of raising the real rate of interest—that is, making it fall less—and thus reducing the value of customers $\hat{q}_x$ by lowering the present discounted value of future profits.

The net impact of the three effects of a decline in λ is then to increase the steady-state normalized capital stock $\tilde{K}$, raise the value of capital q_k, lower the value of a customer normalized by consumption $\hat{q}_x$ and raise markups.

To provide economic intuition using the supply of wealth and demand for assets used in Chaps. 1 and 2, we now develop an analogous figure where households hold two forms of assets: physical capital and the value associated with the firm's stock of customers. We can show the equilibrium where the equilibrium real interest rate is determined by an intersection of a downward-sloping demand-for-assets and an upward-sloping supply-of-assets curve. Defining $\tilde{q}_x \equiv \frac{q_x}{\Lambda}$, we can rewrite Eq. (4.7) by using $C = \Pi_K K$, as follows:

$$r = \frac{-\left(\frac{1}{\eta'(1)}\right)\Pi_K \tilde{K}}{\tilde{q}_x} - \left(\frac{g'(1)}{\eta'(1)}\right) + \lambda + n. \tag{4.9}$$

Noting $\tilde{K} = \frac{\bar{L}}{n+\lambda+\delta}$, we obtain, after rearranging, Eq. (4.10):

$$\tilde{q}_x = \frac{-\left(\frac{1}{\eta'(1)}\right)\Pi_K \bar{L}}{\left[r - \lambda - n + \left(\frac{g'(1)}{\eta'(1)}\right)\right]\left[n+\lambda+\delta\right]}. \tag{4.10}$$

The numerator represents the profits from a customer. This is the relationship between $\tilde{q}_x$ and r in the left-hand quadrant of Fig. 4.2. The upward-sloping supply-of-wealth curve was derived as in Chap. 2. The downward-sloping curve is analogous to the one in Chap. 2, but now we

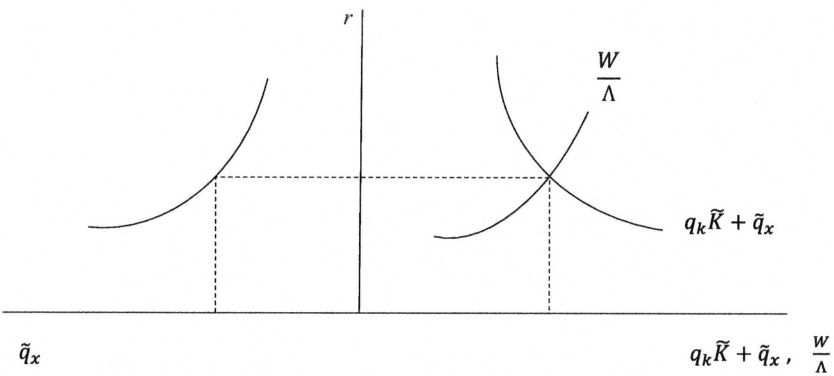

Fig. 4.2 Equilibrium in a two-sector model with customer markets

have introduced markups in the consumer-goods markets, making customers another form of wealth. [2]

We can now use Fig. 4.2 to study the effect of a decline in the rate of productivity growth λ. In essence, the model can be used to explain how the fall in the rate of productivity growth since the early 1970s, documented in the introduction of this book, could have the effect of both causing a booming stock market and a higher share of profits in national income.

As we have shown, the decline in λ leads to a decline in $\hat{q}_x$. Since $\hat{q}_x \equiv \frac{q_x}{C} = \frac{q_x}{\Pi_K K}$, we can rewrite Eq. (4.10) as

$$r-\lambda-n=\frac{-\left(\frac{1}{\eta'(1)}\right)}{\hat{q}_x}-\left(\frac{g'(1)}{\eta'(1)}\right). \tag{4.11}$$

From Eq. (4.11), it follows that although the decline in λ leads to a decline in the real interest rate r, the growth-adjusted real interest rate r - λ rises, and consequently, the price-marginal cost markup is increased. [3] Figure 4.3 shows the effect of a decline in λ.

We show that a decrease in λ leads to a decline in r.

[2] The demand for wealth curve is flatter because of the customer market feature of the consumer-goods sector. When real interest rates fall, the shadow price of customers increases, which makes markups fall, which in turn makes the shadow price of capital q_k increase more than in Chap. 2.

[3] The effect of a change in λ on the real rate of interest r is:

$$\frac{dr}{d\lambda}=\frac{1-\left[\frac{(n+\theta)(\rho+\theta)\left(\frac{1}{\eta'(1)}\right)}{\left(r-\lambda-n+\frac{g'(1)}{\eta'(1)}\right)^2}\right]}{1+\frac{(n+\theta)(\rho+\theta)}{(r+\delta)^2}-\frac{(n+\theta)(\rho+\theta)\left(\frac{1}{\eta'(1)}\right)\left(1-\frac{\Psi'(\hat{q}_x)}{(r+\delta)\Psi^2}\right)}{\left(r-\lambda-n+\frac{g'(1)}{\eta'(1)}\right)^2}}>0.$$

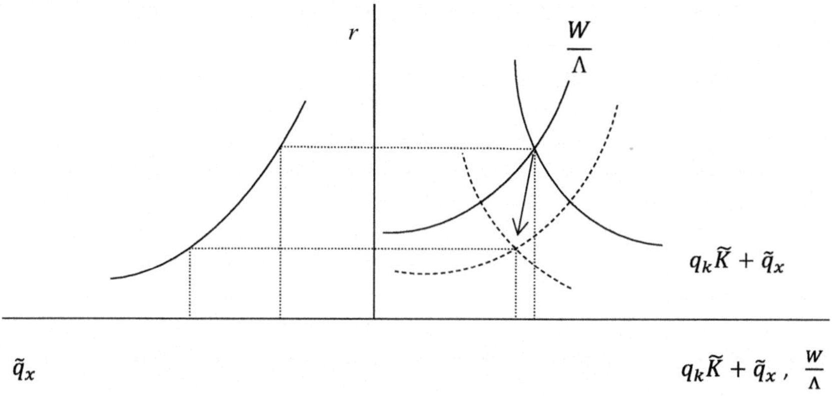

Fig. 4.3 Effect of a fall in productivity growth

The upward-sloping supply-of-wealth curve shifts to the right. Intuitively, weaker productivity growth reduces future wage growth and lowers the level of human capital, which increases the saving of individuals, hence the supply of nonhuman wealth at each rate of interest. As the real rate of interest falls, we move down the demand-for-wealth curve where the normalized price of customers, $\tilde{q}_x$, rises. In addition, there are two effects of the productivity slowdown on the position of the downward-sloping demand-for-wealth curve. First the fall in λ lowers the normalized value of customers through a discounting effect, which makes the curve shift to the left. A lower $\tilde{q}_x$ also raises markups, which makes q_k fall, reinforcing the leftward shift. But there is an offsetting effect working through $\tilde{K}$, which raises $\tilde{q}_x$, and the change in $q_k\tilde{K}$ is ambiguous at a given interest rate because while q_k falls unambiguously, $\tilde{K}$ rises. Finally, there is an ambiguous effect on the position of the curve in the left-hand quadrant of the graph.[4]

We can summarize the effect of a decline in productivity growth as follows: individuals, anticipating slower growth of future wages, save more, which lowers the equilibrium real rate of interest and raises $\tilde{q}_x$. At the same time, the lower rate of growth of productivity makes the normalized shadow price of customers $\tilde{q}_x$ fall at a given real rate of interest, which

[4] One effect of a fall in λ is to decrease the present discounted value of future markups, which shifts the curve to the right. Another is to increase the steady-state normalized level of capital, which shifts it to the left by increasing the stream of profits associated with a customer.

lowers the demand for wealth and lowers the real rate of interest further. The effect is to raise markups of price over marginal cost.

Without going through a formal derivation, we can describe the effect of a fall in the rate of population growth n. A fall in population growth lowers consumption demand through a lower value of $\tilde{q}_x$, market share being less valuable when the population is expected to increase at a slower rate. This reduces the return on customers—in particular, the capital gain on expanding the customer base. To put it simply, having a larger market share is less valuable when the size of the market is expected to grow more slowly than before.

Returning to the golden rule of Phelps (1961) shown in Eq. (4.3), which shows the relationship between the rental of capital $r + \delta$ and the rate of return on capital Π_K/q_k, a fall in either productivity growth λ or population growth n has the effect of raising markups and increasing the divergence between the rental of capital and the return on capital, creating the illusion of dynamic inefficiency, when in fact the capital stock is below the golden rule level. To repeat, a low real rate of interest does not have to imply dynamic inefficiency so that increased public debt may lower output and consumption even when real interest rates are close to zero. We now describe the effect of higher debt on the stock of capital.

4.3 A Helicopter Drop of Public Debt

We now introduce public debt as in Chap. 2. Due to the Blanchard-Buiter-Weil setup, debt appears with other assets in the economy: capital and the customer base. Debt $\hat{D} \equiv D/C$ now appears in the asset-pricing relationship, Eq. (4.5'):

$$\left\{\rho+(n+\theta)(\rho+\theta)\left(\hat{q}_x+\hat{D}+\frac{q_k}{\Pi_K}\right)+\frac{\bar{L}}{\tilde{K}}-n\right\}q_k=\frac{\Pi_K}{\Psi(\hat{q}_x)}. \tag{4.5'}$$

The equation gives a positively-sloped schedule relating q_k to $\tilde{K}$, reflecting the negative effect of higher $\tilde{K}$ on the rental for capital and the real rate of interest, which then raises q_k. A rise in wealth, because of either a rise in the value of customers $\hat{q}_x$ or a rise in the level of debt $\hat{D}$, increases the rate of interest, lowering q_k and shifting the upward-sloping relationship in the q_k to $\tilde{K}$ plane to the right. There is also a negative effect of higher real interest rates on $\hat{q}_x$, as is seen in Eq. (4.11), operating through

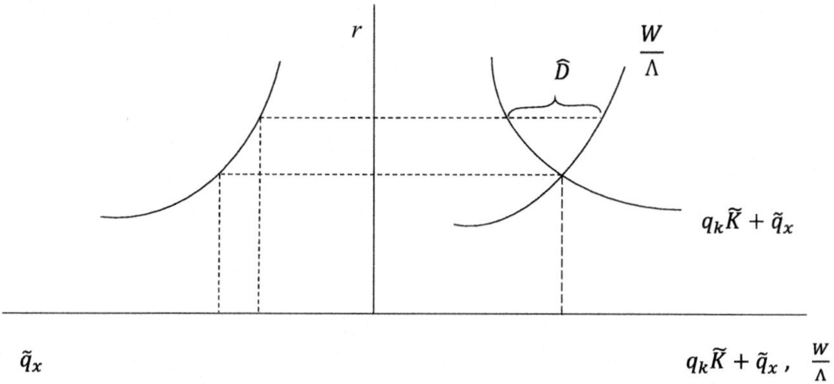

Fig. 4.4 Effect of public debt in the two-sector model

lower markups on the value of capital, shifting the schedule to the left because lower markups increase the return on physical capital, as the owner of the capital stock receives a larger share of output. The new dimension here is the effect of an increase in the level of debt on the schedule, which makes the curve shift to the right.

When the level of debt rises, it increases the supply of wealth in Fig. 4.4, creating a wedge between the demand for capital and customers and the supply of wealth. The effect is to raise the real interest rate, which then lowers the value of customers q_x, $\tilde{q}_x$, as well as $\hat{q}_x$ and q_k.[5] From Eq. (4.11), the higher interest rate lowers $\hat{q}_x$ due to a discounting effect, which raises markups, making q_k fall further, as is shown in Eq. (4.3).

In Fig. 4.5, the increase in debt has the effect of shifting the upward-sloping asset-price relationship for capital in the right-hand quadrant, Eq. (4.5'), to the right, lowering the shadow value of capital q_k. In the left-hand quadrant, the relationship between $\hat{q}_x$ and q_k is also affected by the introduction of public debt. Equation (4.8) now becomes

[5] There is also the effect of lower consumption per customer C on $\hat{q}_x$, but it is smaller than the effect of a fall in q_x.

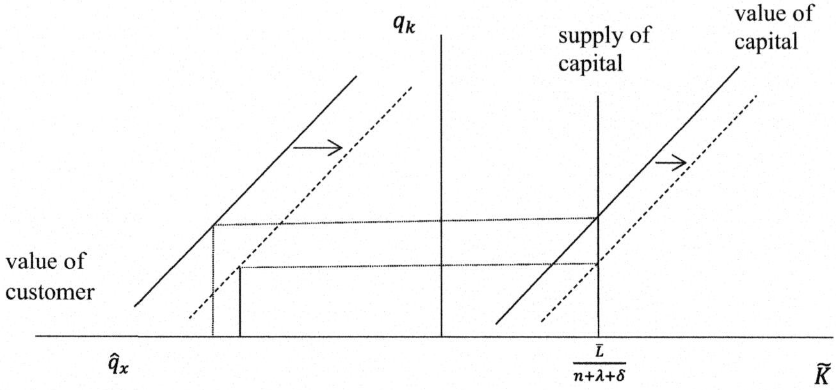

Fig. 4.5 An increase in public debt

$$\left\{\rho+(n+\theta)(\rho+\theta)\left(\hat{q}_x+\hat{D}+\frac{q_k}{\Pi_K}\right)+\left[\frac{g'(1)}{\eta'(1)}\right]-n\right\}\hat{q}_x=\frac{-1}{\eta'(1)}, \quad (4.8')$$

which is a negative relationship between $\hat{q}_x$ and q_k. In effect, a higher q_k increases the real rate of interest through a wealth effect on consumption, which lowers the shadow price of customers as shown in Eq. (4.6). An increase in debt $\hat{D}$ will shift the downward-sloping curve to the right, giving a lower value of $\hat{q}_x$ for every level of q_k. The effect is to lower both q_k and $\hat{q}_x$, while leaving the stock of capital $\tilde{K}$ unchanged. As in Chap. 1, we find that the stock of capital measured in units of consumer goods falls.

We can now return to our earlier results on the golden rule. The increased public debt has had the effect of raising the real rate of interest and lowering the value of capital. In the absence of markups of price over marginal cost, this would be welfare-improving, starting from a position where $r < \lambda + n$, but with markups, as is shown in Eq. (4.3), this inequality does not have to imply dynamic inefficiency. Increased debt may therefore lower steady-state consumption also when real interest rates are lower than the steady-state growth rate of the economy.

4.4 Transitional Dynamics

The analysis hitherto has been confined to steady-state equilibria. We now turn to transitional dynamics to show how the decline in λ can lead to a gradual and steady rise in markups and the shadow price of capital, that is, rising share of profits and rising stock prices.

The full system of dynamic equations is given by

$$\dot{\tilde{K}} = \bar{L} - (n + \lambda + \delta)\tilde{K}, \tag{4.12}$$

$$\dot{q}_k = \left\{ \rho + (n+\theta)(\rho+\theta)\left(\hat{q}_x + \frac{q_k}{\Pi_K} \right) + \frac{\bar{L}}{\tilde{K}} - n \right\} q_k - \frac{\Pi_K}{\Psi(\hat{q}_x)}, \tag{4.13}$$

$$\dot{\hat{q}}_x = \left\{ \rho + (n+\theta)(\rho+\theta)\left(\hat{q}_x + \frac{q_k}{\Pi_K} \right) + \left[\frac{g'(1)}{\eta'(1)} \right] - n \right\} \hat{q}_x + \frac{1}{\eta'(1)}. \tag{4.14}$$

Linearizing around the steady state, the system of equations given by Eqs. (4.12) to (4.14) can be expressed as

$$\dot{\tilde{K}} = -(n + \lambda + \delta)\left(\tilde{K} - \tilde{K}_{ss}\right), \tag{4.15}$$

$$\begin{aligned} \dot{q}_k = {} & \frac{-q_k \bar{L}}{\tilde{K}^2}\left(\tilde{K} - \tilde{K}_{ss}\right) + \left\{ \rho + (n+\theta)(\rho+\theta)\left(\hat{q}_x + \frac{2q_k}{\Pi_K} \right) + \frac{\bar{L}}{\tilde{K}} - n \right\}\left(q_k - q_{k,ss}\right) \\ & + \left\{ \rho + (n+\theta)(\rho+\theta) q_k + \frac{\Pi_K \Psi'(\hat{q}_x)}{\left(\Psi(\hat{q}_x)\right)^2} \right\}\left(\hat{q}_x - \hat{q}_{x,ss}\right) \end{aligned}, \tag{4.16}$$

$$\begin{aligned} \dot{\hat{q}}_x = {} & \left\{ \rho + \frac{(n+\theta)(\rho+\theta)\hat{q}_x}{\Pi_K} \right\}\left(q_k - q_{k,ss}\right) \\ & + \left\{ \rho + (n+\theta)(\rho+\theta)\left(2\hat{q}_x + \frac{q_k}{\Pi_K} \right) + \left[\frac{g'(1)}{\eta'(1)} \right] - n \right\}\left(\hat{q}_x - \hat{q}_{x,ss}\right). \end{aligned} \tag{4.17}$$

The conditions under which the system represented by Eqs. (4.15), (4.16), and (4.17) exhibit stable adjustment paths are shown in the appendix to this chapter. The eigenvalues of the linearized system are μ_1, μ_2, and μ_3 such that $\mu_1 < 0$, $\mu_2 > 0$ and $\mu_3 > 0$. We can write

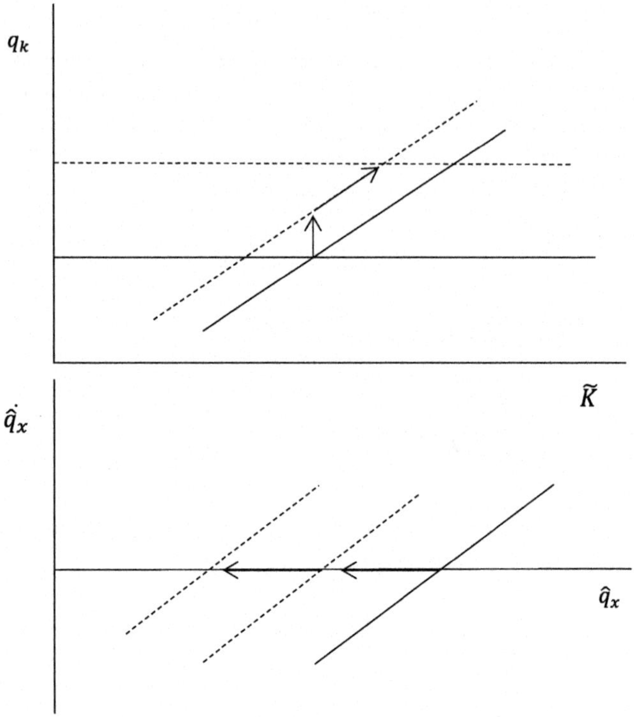

Fig. 4.6 Transitional dynamics in response to a decline in λ

$$\tilde{K}_t = \tilde{K}_{ss} + \left(\tilde{K}_0 - \tilde{K}_{ss}\right)e^{\mu_1 t} \tag{4.18}$$

$$q_{k,t} = q_{k,ss} + \left(\frac{a_{21}}{\mu_1 - a_{22}}\right)\left(\tilde{K}_0 - \tilde{K}_{ss}\right)e^{\mu_1 t}, \tag{4.19}$$

where $a_{21} < 0$ and $a_{22} > 0$ are defined in the appendix, which explains why the linear relationship between q_k and $\tilde{K}$ in the top half of Fig. 4.3 is positively sloped. The bottom half of Fig. 4.6 shows a positive relationship between $\hat{q}_x$ and $\hat{q}_x$ for a given q_k. An increase in q_k shifts this curve upwards.

The analysis of the system of equations shows that when the rate of labor-augmenting technical progress, λ, declines, the rise in the shadow price of a unit of capital, q_k, is gradual after the initial jump, as is shown in the top half of Fig. 4.6. Along the transition path to the new steady state, $\hat{q}_x$ gradually declines after an initial drop. Correspondingly, since the markup is negatively related to $\hat{q}_x$, it rises gradually after an initial jump.

4.5 Conclusions

We have used the customer-market model of Phelps and Winter (1970) in a two-sector model to explain the rising share of profits in national income and the corresponding fall in the share of wages.

We show how weaker productivity growth leads to a jump in steady-state consumption due to a rise in the price of capital. There are two countervailing effects on markups. First, the weaker expected productivity growth makes real interest rates fall, thus increasing the value of a customer, which would make firms want to decrease markups in order to increase their market share. But the increase in current consumption increases the marginal benefit of raising markups due to the larger volume of sales, and it is this effect that dominates. Raising prices increases current profits, and this influences the representative firm's decision more than the expected loss of market share.

When the rate of population growth declines, the market share becomes less valuable, which also makes firms raise their markups. This reduces the return on customers—in particular, the capital gain on expanding the customer base. Thus, the decline in both the rate of productivity growth and the rate of growth of population has the effect of both raising the price of capital and raising markups.

Higher markups then raise the share of profits as a share of national income, which is consistent with the stylized facts of a booming stock market and a rising share of profits in national income observed in the US. Moreover, by raising markups, a fall in either productivity growth or population growth has the effect of increasing the divergence between the rental of capital and the return on capital, creating the illusion of dynamic inefficiency, when in fact the capital stock is below the golden rule level. Therefore, a low real rate of interest does not have to imply dynamic inefficiency, so that increased public debt may lower output and consumption even when real interest rates are close to zero.

Appendix

We linearize the dynamic equations given by Eqs. (4.12), (4.13), and (4.14) around the steady-state equilibrium. The linearized dynamic system around the steady state $\left(\tilde{K}_{ss}, q_{k,ss}, \hat{q}_{x,ss}\right)$ is given by

$$\left[\dot{\tilde{K}}, \dot{q}_k, \dot{\hat{q}}_x\right]' = A\left[\tilde{K}-\tilde{K}_{ss}, q_k - q_{k,ss}, \hat{q}_x - \hat{q}_{x,ss}\right]',$$

where $[\cdots]'$ denotes a column vector, and the 3×3 matrix A contains the following elements:

$$a_{11} = -\left(n+\lambda-\delta\right) < 0,$$

$$a_{11} = 0,$$

$$a_{13} = 0,$$

$$a_{21} = \frac{-\bar{L}q_{k,ss}}{\tilde{K}_{ss}^{2}} < 0,$$

$$a_{22} = \left\{\rho + (n+\theta)(\rho+\theta)\left(\hat{q}_{x,ss} + \frac{2q_{k,ss}}{\Pi_K}\right) - n + \frac{\bar{L}}{\tilde{K}_{ss}}\right\} > 0,$$

$$a_{23} = \left\{\rho + (n+\theta)(\rho+\theta)q_{k,ss} + \frac{\Pi_K \Psi'\left(\hat{q}_{x,ss}\right)}{\Psi^2}\right\} < 0,$$

$$a_{31} = 0,$$

$$a_{32} = \rho + \frac{(n+\theta)(\rho+\theta)\hat{q}_{x,ss}}{\Pi_K} > 0,$$

$$a_{33} = \left\{\rho + (n+\theta)(\rho+\theta)\left(2\hat{q}_{x,ss} + \frac{q_{k,ss}}{\Pi_K}\right) + \left[\frac{g'(1)}{\eta'(1)}\right] - n\right\} > 0.$$

The determinant of A, $Det(A) = a_{11}a_{22}a_{33} - a_{11}a_{32}a_{23}$, is negative. We assume that the trace of A, $Trace(A) = a_{11} + a_{22} + a_{33}$, is positive. The product of the roots of the system is given by the determinant, while the sum of the roots gives the trace. Since the determinant is negative, this establishes whether there are three negative roots or one. A necessary condition for stability of a 3 ×3 system is that the trace of the matrix A must be negative. Since we have assumed that *Trace*(A) is positive, accordingly, the dynamic system represented by Eqs. (4.15–4.17) is unstable, implying that it has at least one positive root. Because we know it has either zero or two positive roots, it must have two. There is therefore a unique negative root and a unique perfect foresight path that converges to the steady state.

References

Ball, L. M., & Mankiw, N. G. (2023). Market power in neoclassical growth models, *Review of Economic Studies, 90*(2), 572–596.

De Loecker, J., Eeckhout, J., & Unger, G. (2020). The rise of market power and the macroeconomic implications. *Quarterly Journal of Economics, 135*(2), 561–644.

Mankiw, N. G. (2022). *Government debt and capital accumulation in an era of low interest rates.* NBER Working Paper 30024.

Phelps, E. S. (1961). The golden rule of accumulation: A fable for growthmen. *American Economic Review, 51*(4), 638–643.

Phelps, E. S., & Winter, S. (1970). Optimal price policy under atomistic competition. In E. S. Phelps et al. (Eds.), *Microeconomic foundations of employment and inflation theory* (pp. 309–337). New York: W.W. Norton.

CHAPTER 5

The Slowdown in the Data

In previous chapters, we have shown how falling rates of productivity growth make real interest rates fall and share prices and markups increase. We have attributed the fall in interest rates to changes on the supply side of the economy because the decline in the real interest rate has occurred over a period of more than four decades.

In the one-sector neoclassical model, derived in Chap. 2, a fall in the rate of productivity growth had the effect of raising the supply of saving, lowering the equilibrium real rate of interest, and increasing the normalized capital stock and the normalized level of wealth. Moreover, a fall in the rate of population growth also had the effect of lowering real interest rates. In contrast, an increase in government debt raised the real interest rate by increasing household wealth and creating a wedge between wealth and the stock of capital. The stock of capital normalized by productivity was reduced. In Chap. 3, we showed that the fall in the rate of productivity growth had the effect of raising the shadow price of capital through lower interest rates, thereby leading to higher stock prices. In Chap. 4, we showed that markups and the share of profits in income also increase when the rate of productivity growth falls because firms expect consumption per customer to rise less rapidly, making customers less valuable to firms.

We begin by mapping the patterns in the data. Using principal components analysis, we show the pattern of changes in our causal variables—productivity growth rates, population growth, and government debt—and

E. Phelps et al., *The Great Economic Slowdown*,
https://doi.org/10.1007/978-3-031-31441-4_5

then the patterns in the variables endogenous to our model—real interest rate, investment, share prices, profit shares, labor participation, and employment. We next analyze the evolution of real interest rates in the past seven decades, the extent to which they move together across the G7 countries before turning to explain the fall in real rates by the slowdown of productivity growth. This we do by estimating a Taylor equation, which has an endogenous equilibrium rate of interest that depends on productivity growth, population growth, debt, and a measure of labor supply. Then we use historical data series that go back to the 1920s to explore the effect of productivity growth, population growth, and government debt on the rate of return to equity and housing, investment, real wage growth, and employment using an error-correction equation with fixed effects. The following section describes the evolution of markups and share prices and the chapter's last section describes the evidence on job satisfaction.

5.1 Patterns in the Data

We use the historical database of Jorda, Schularick, and Taylor (2019) (JST), as well as data collected by the Bank of France on total factor productivity growth over the long run (see Bergeaud et al., 2022). We first use principal component analysis to find the common pattern in each series for the G7 countries and then a fixed-effects estimator to measure the effect of the slowdown of productivity growth on equilibrium interest rates, share prices, markups, investment, and employment.

We start by showing the H-P filtered series for the rate of productivity growth for the US. There was a slowdown in productivity growth in the early 1970s, a temporary rebound in the late 1990s, and then a return to weak growth (Fig. 5.1).

We want to identify whether a common story is taking place in the different G7 countries. We take the matrix of TFP growth in each country from 1950 to 2019, population growth, the level of public debt as a ratio to GDP, real interest rates, gross capital formation as a share of GDP, share prices normalized by productivity, the share of profits in GDP (source: Eeckhout, 2022a), male labor force participation, the unemployment rate, and real wages (source: OECD), and then calculate the principal components (PC) of each matrix to summarize developments in the G7. If there is a common story, the first principal components would explain a large fraction of the variation in each variable, and there would be a roughly equal weight for each country in the eigenvectors.

To start with, we take a look at the first two PCs for the three causal variables in our models: TFP growth, population growth, and government debt (Tables 5.1 and 5.2).

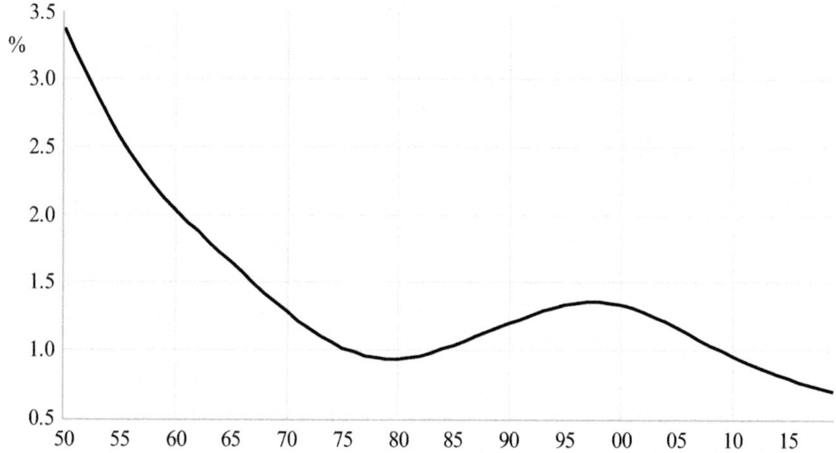

Fig. 5.1 TFP productivity growth in the US. Source: Bergeaud et al. (2022) at the Bank of France. The series has been smoothed using the Hodrick-Prescott filter with a smoothing parameter equal to 1600

Table 5.1 Eigenvalues for causal variables (1950–2019)

	Value	*Proportion*	*Cumulative proportion*
TFP growth (%)			
First PC	3.8	0.54	0.54
Second PC	1.0	0.14	0.68
Population growth (%)			
First PC	3.7	0.52	0.52
Second PC	1.5	0.21	0.74
Public debt (% of GDP)			
First PC	5.1	0.72	0.72
Second PC	1.5	0.21	0.93

Note: The German population growth series omits the observation for 1991, when the former GDR was incorporated into the BRD

The first PC explains 54% of the variation across the seven countries over the sample period for TFP growth. It explains 52% for population growth and 72% for public debt.

The eigenvectors for the first PC for each of the variables have positive values for each of the seven countries, with the exception of the UK for public debt. This reflects the declining ratio of debt to GDP in the UK in the 1960s and 1970s. The zero value for the UK in the eigenvector for

Table 5.2 Eigenvectors for causal variables (1950–2019)

	TFP growth		*Population growth*		*Public debt*	
	PC1	*PC2*	*PC1*	*PC2*	*PC1*	*PC2*
Canada	0.38	-0.16	0.43	-0.14	0.36	0.21
France	0.42	0.07	0.43	-0.07	0.43	0.12
Germany	0.41	0.18	0.33	0.42	0.43	-0.17
Italy	0.44	-0.23	0.39	0.32	0.42	-0.23
Japan	0.42	0.14	0.43	-0.27	0.43	-0.09
UK	0.17	0.83	0.02	0.77	-0.11	0.79
US	0.33	-0.42	0.44	-0.16	0.36	0.47

population growth reflects more robust population growth in the UK over the past 40 years.

The second PC for TFP growth captures the late-1990s pickup in productivity growth in the US, which then petered out after the turn of the century. The second PC for population growth shows the more robust population growth in the UK since the early 1980s and the large increase in 2017. The second PC for public debt captures the declining public debt in the UK in the 1960s and 1970s and the greater increase in public debt in the UK following the financial crisis.

Figure 5.2 shows the first PCs for the three causal variables. The PC for productivity growth shows the general slowdown of productivity growth in the G7 countries since the 1950s. There is also a decline in population growth from the baby boom of the postwar era onward. Finally, we can see the general increase in public debt as a share of GDP since the beginning of the 1980s, with a big jump following the financial crisis in 2008.

Next we turn to the consequences of the great slowdown. Table 5.3 shows the eigenvalues for real interest rates, investment, share prices (normalized by total factor productivity), the share of profits in GDP, male labor force participation, unemployment, and real wages. Of the seven variables, five have a first principal component that explains more than 50% of the variation in the data.[1]

[1] Onatski and Wang (2021) warn that principal component analysis can be misleading in nonstationary data. They suggest that the time series plots of the extracted factors should be analyzed in order to detect spurious factors. In particular, a resemblance to cosine waves should raise the alarm. This is not the case for our estimated principal components.

Fig. 5.2 The first PCs for TFP growth, population growth, and public debt

Table 5.3 Eigenvalues for derived variables

	Value	*Proportion*	*Cumulative proportion*
Real rate of interest (%)			
First PC	4.5	0.66	0.66
Second PC	0.9	0.14	0.80
Investment (% of GDP)			
First PC	3.0	0.42	0.42
Second PC	1.7	0.25	0.67
Share prices			
First PC	4.2	0.59	0.59
Second PC	1.5	0.21	0.80
Share of profits in GDP (%)			
First PC	2.7	0.39	0.39
Second PC	1.8	0.25	0.64
Third PC*	1.5	0.21	0.85
Male labor participation (%)			
First PC	4.6	0.66	0.66
Second PC	1.3	0.19	0.85
Unemployment (%)			
First PC	4.3	0.61	0.61
Second PC	1.6	0.23	0.84
Real wages			
First PC	6.4	0.92	0.92
Second PC	0.4	0.05	0.97

* Fourth eigenvalue is equal to 0.07

The real rate of interest has a first PC that explains 66% of the variation with a corresponding eigenvector, shown in Table 5.4, that has positive values for all seven countries. This suggests that real interest rates move together across the countries. The real interest rate rose at the beginning of the 1980s and has been declining since then across the G7 countries.

The first PC for investment explains 42% of the variation in the investment matrix and has a positive value in the eigenvector for the countries in Europe and Japan, where investment fell in the 1970s, 1980s, and 1990s. The second PC shows the investment boom in the US from 1990 to 2010, the subsequent fall, and then the recovery.

The first PC for normalized share prices shows the fall in the stock market in the 1970s, the rise since the early 1980s in all seven countries, and the slumps during the early 2000s and the 2008 financial crisis.

Table 5.4 Eigenvectors for derived variables

Country	*Real rate*		*Investment*		*Share prices*		*Profit share*		*Participation*		*Unemployment*		*Real wages*	
	PC1	*PC2*	*PC1*	*PC2*	*PC1*	*PC2*	*PC1*	*PC2*	*PC1*	*PC2*	*PC1*	*PC2*	*PC1*	*PC2*
Canada	0.42	-0.28	0.09	0.54	0.39	-0.42	0.54	-0.09	0.44	0.14	0.39	0.39	0.39	-0.16
France	0.38	-0.38	0.32	0.55	0.45	0.30	-0.02	0.51	0.36	0.41	0.45	-0.14	0.39	0.01
Germany	0.32	0.47	0.47	-0.06	0.46	0.19	0.40	0.32	-0.20	0.72	0.42	-0.26	0.39	0.02
Italy	0.39	0.16	0.49	0.14	0.21	0.73	0.04	-0.47	0.38	0.32	0.37	-0.38	039	0.16
Japan	0.33	0.63	0.50	-0.31	0.05	0.06	-0.40	0.45	-0.39	0.02	0.36	-0.34	0.35	0.76
UK	0.37	-0.37	0.33	-0.48	0.44	-0.12	-0.27	-0.46	0.44	-0.05	0.40	0.38	0.37	-0.15
US	0.42	-0.05	-0.27	-0.21	0.43	-0.39	0.56	0.01	0.38	-0.44	0.22	0.60	0.36	-0.60

The first PC for the profit share captures its rise in Canada and the US since the early 1970s and explains 39% of the variation. The second PC captures the fall in France and Japan in the 1970s. The third PC captures the changes in the profit share on the European continent, rising in the 1980s and falling since then back to the same level.

The first PC for male labor force participation captures the decline since at least the early 1970s in the US, as well as in Italy; since the early 1990s in the UK and Canada; and since the 1980s in France. Unemployment has a first PC with positive values for all countries in the corresponding eigenvector, explaining 61% of the variation in the data. It captures the rise in unemployment in the G7 in the 1970s and early 1980s and the business cycle through the early-1990s recession to the 2008 financial crisis. The second PC then captures the recovery of unemployment in the US, the UK, and Canada in the late 1980s and 1990s, and the simultaneous further increase in Europe and Japan.

The first PC for real wages explains 92% of the variation in the matrix. The eigenvector has a positive weight on each country. The PC captures the rise in real wages until the 1970s and the stagnation thereafter.

The seven PCs are shown in Fig. 5.3.

The slowdown of productivity growth and population growth shown in Fig. 5.2 goes together with declining real interest rates, declining investment as a share of GDP, rising share prices, a rising share of profits in GDP, declining male labor force participation, rising unemployment, and stagnating real wages.

5.2 Real Interest Rates

We denote the nominal interest rate by i, the real rate by r, the average of the G7 real rate of interest by r^*, the level of debt as a ratio to GDP by D, the rate of growth of productivity by λ, and the real wage by v. The *ex post* real rate of interest is defined as

$$r_{it} = \frac{1+i_{it}}{1+\pi_{it}} - 1,$$

where π is the rate of inflation, $\Delta logP$, where P is the consumer price index.

Table 5.5 shows the descriptive statistics for the variables used to calculate real interest rates. These are nominal interest rates (short and long), real interest rates (short and long), the average of these interest rates across

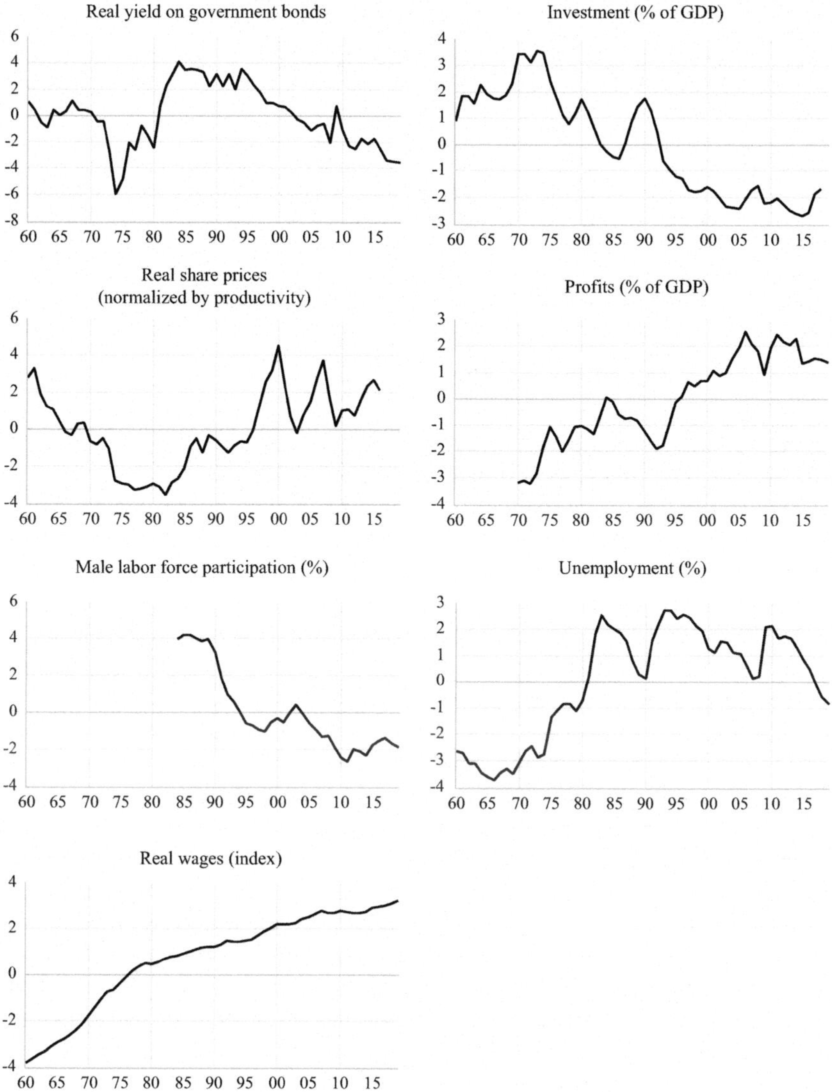

Fig. 5.3 The first principal components of the affected variables

Table 5.5 Descriptive statistics, percentages (1950–2019)

	i_s	i_s^*	i_l	i_l^*	π	r_s
Mean	5.12	5.09	6.27	6.43	3.73	1.37
SD	3.95	3.40	3.39	3.04	3.75	2.81
Min	-0.74	0.01	-0.25	0.91	-7.11	-11.02
Max	19.70	14.40	20.22	13.39	21.94	11.47
	r_s^*	r_l	r_l^*	D/Y	λ	
Mean	1.35	2.50	2.50	0.65	1.75	
SD	2.25	2.66	2.09	0.44	2.13	
Min	-6.80	-10.40	-5.65	0.04	-3.79	
Max	5.60	13.58	5.91	2.39	13.17	

the G7 countries i^* and r^*, respectively, the rate of growth of total factor productivity (λ), and the ratio of government debt to GDP (D).

Due to the variability of inflation, which has a maximum value of 21.9% and a minimum value of -7.1%, the real rate of interest has a low minimum, or -11.0% for the short rate and -10.4% for the long rate.

Inflation has been low and relatively stable in the G7 countries since the early 1990s, and for that reason the path of nominal interest rates in the three decades since the beginning of the 1990s shows how equilibrium interest rates have fallen more accurately than the volatile *ex post* real interest rates do. Figure 5.4 shows the nominal yield on long government debt for the G7 countries. In France and Germany there has been a continuous downward movement of nominal interest rates from 1990 to 2019. In Italy, the trend is also downward, but we note a sudden drop when Italy entered the eurozone in 1999, as nominal interest rates fell from around 12% to around 5% with the adoption of the euro. In Japan, the financial crisis of 1990 triggered a rapid fall in interest rates, which then fell again in the 2010s. Interest rates in the US trended downwards over the entire period, reaching a minimum of around 2% in the mid-2010s. In the UK as well, interest rates have fallen over the period, although there was an uptick in the middle of the 1990s, when interest rates rose during an economic boom and then resumed their downward path.

Both the nominal rate of interest and the real rate of interest are related across countries in both short and long run because of capital market

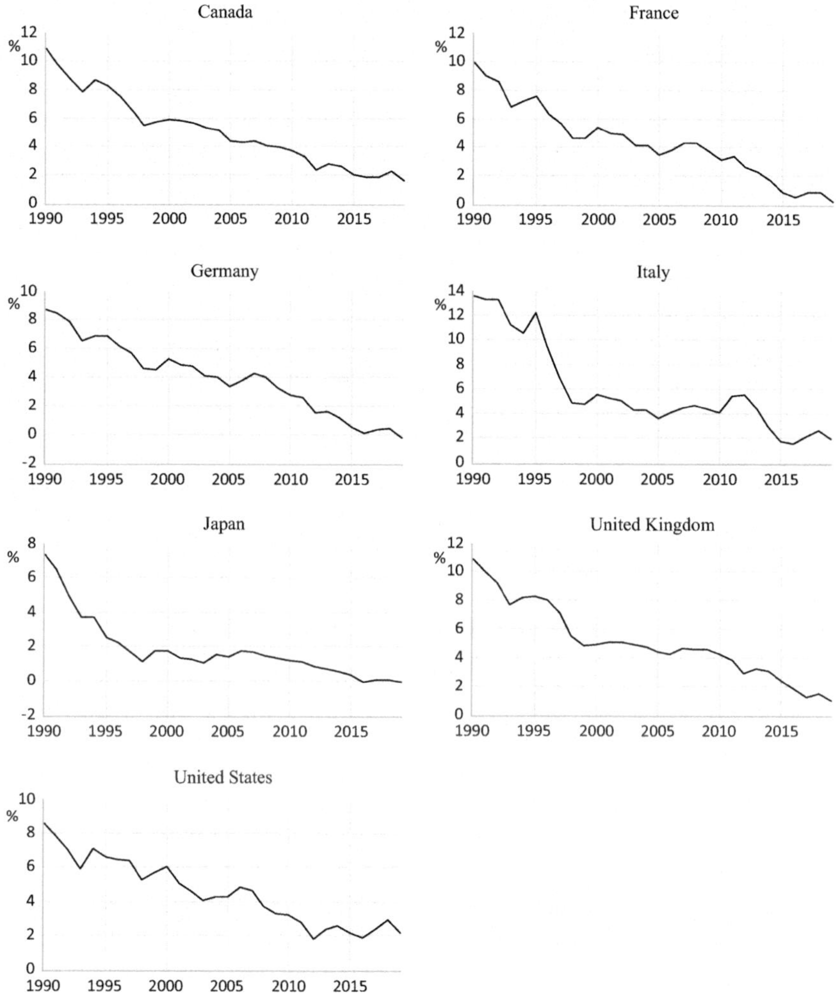

Fig. 5.4 The yield on long (10-year) government bonds in G7 countries

integration. The following equation measures the short-run and long-run relationship between the *long* real rate of interest and the average real rate in a panel of the G7 countries (t-statistics in parentheses) using data from 1950 to 2019.

$$\Delta(r_{lit}) = -0.00 + \underset{(0.03)}{} \underset{(24.90)}{1.00}\ \Delta(\bar{r}_{lt}) + \underset{(14.14)}{0.77}\ \bar{r}_{lt-1} - \underset{(18.62)}{0.77}\ r_{lit-1} - \underset{(0.48)}{0.01}\ \Delta(r_{lit-1}) + u_{it} \quad (5.1)$$

The short-run effect of a change in the average real rate is equal to one, and there is also a long-run effect equal to one. The equation explains more than half of the variation in the data (R-squared is equal to 0.72).[2]

The short-run real rates are also linked across countries. The following equation shows the short-run and long-run relationship between the *short* real rate of interest (on one-year government bonds) and its average in a panel of the G7 countries[3]:

$$\Delta(r_{sit}) = -0.04 + \underset{(0.58)}{} \underset{(19.82)}{1.00}\ \Delta(\bar{r}_{st}) + \underset{(10.24)}{0.47}\ \bar{r}_{st-1} - \underset{(12.27)}{0.46}\ r_{sit-1} - \underset{(1.48)}{-0.04}\ \Delta(r_{sit-1}) + u_{it} \quad (5.2)$$

Again, the effect of a change in the average real rate is equal to one, and there is also a long-run relationship equal to one. The equation explains half of the variation in the data (R-squared is equal to 0.59).

5.3 Augmented Taylor Rule Equation

To show how declining productivity growth and population growth rates can explain falling real rates of interest, the following Taylor rule equation was estimated for the G7 countries from 1950 to 2019, where the equilibrium real rate of interest is made a function of the variables shown in previous chapters to affect it; namely, productivity growth λ, population growth n, public debt D (as a share of GDP), and a proxy for the supply of labor by each worker $\bar{L}$:

$$r_{sit} \equiv i^{*}_{sit} - \pi_{it} = r^{*}_{sit}\left(\lambda_{it}, D_{it}, n_{it}, \bar{L}_{it}\right) + \alpha\left(u_{it} - u^{*}_{it}\right) + \beta\left(\pi_{it} - \pi^{*}\right) + u_{it} \quad (5.3)$$

The equation has short real rates as a function of the equilibrium short real rate, the deviation of unemployment from its natural rate and the deviation of inflation from 2.5%, which we take as a target rate. Then the

[2] The finding that the average interest rates over the 17 countries do a good job explaining the change in national interest rates, which implies that the national rates move together, is in line with the results of Del Negro et al. (2019) and Rachel and Summers (2019).

[3] Estimated with a fixed-effects estimator.

equilibrium real rate r^* is a function of the rate of growth of productivity (λ), public debt (D), and demographic variables, in particular the rate of growth of the population (n) and labor supply ($\bar{L}$), all in line with the theoretical models presented in previous chapters. We use the Hodrick-Prescott filter to derive time series that proxy for the natural rate of unemployment u^* for each of the G7 countries from the seven unemployment rate series.[4]

The results of the estimation are shown in Table 5.6. In column (1), we use data for the G7 countries from 1950 to 2019 to estimate the effect of inflation and unemployment on the (*ex post*) short-term real interest rate using pooled data. The results show that higher unemployment gives lower real interest rates and that when inflation goes up the real interest rate falls, but by less than the rise in inflation—a one percentage increase in inflation makes the real interest rate fall by 0.12%. In contrast, the Taylor rule would suggest that central banks raise real interest rates by 0.50% for each 1% increase in inflation. The explanatory power of the equation is very weak. In column (2), we use the fixed-effect estimator, and the results are almost identical.

Also in column (3), we show results of a pooled regression where the equilibrium real rate of interest r^* is a function of the rate of growth of productivity λ, public debt D, the population between ages 20 and 24 as a share of the total population, and the working-age population (15–64) as a share of the total population. We use the share of young workers as a proxy for the rate of population growth, which had a positive effect on the real rate of interest in the model presented in Chaps. 2, 3, and 4. We use the share of the working-age population as a proxy for the time endowment variable $\bar{L}$ in Chap. 2, which had the effect of increasing the demand for capital, the supply of wealth, and the equilibrium levels of capital and wealth, with an ambiguous effect on the real rate of interest. In column (3), we find that a one percentage point increase in inflation makes the real rate of interest fall by 0.28%, and an increase in unemployment by one percentage makes the real rate fall by 0.55%. While the latter effect is consistent with the Taylor rule, the former again implies that nominal rates rise

[4] There is clearly an endogeneity issue associated with using inflation and unemployment to explain interest rates. However, while central banks respond (or should respond) quickly to changes in unemployment and inflation, their effect on the two variables only happens with a long lag. The effect of current interest rates on inflation takes over two years to have its full impact, while the effect on output and employment on interest rates takes about one year, according to Christiano et al. (1996).

Table 5.6 Estimation of augmented Taylor equations

Dependent variable	*Short-term real interest rate*				*Short-term nominal interest rate*			
	1960–2019				*1960–2019*			
	(1)	*(2)*	*(3)*	*(4)*	*(5)*	*(6)*	*(7)*	*(8)*
	Pooled	*F.E.*	*Pooled*	*F.E.*	*Pooled*	*F.E.*	*Pooled*	*F.E.*
Constant	1.63***	1.65***	-17.72***	-30.00***	4.20***	4.21***	-15.84***	28.47***
	(12.7)	(12.7)	(5.0)	(6.2)	(20.8)	(30.8)	(4.2)	(5.6)
π - 2.5	-0.12***	-0.13***	-0.28***	-0.41***	0.87***	0.86***	0.71***	0.56***
	(3.6)	(3.8)	(6.6)	(8.9)	(24.5)	(23.3)	(15.9)	(11.5)
u - u*	-0.28*	-0.29**	-0.55***	-0.67***	-0.30*	-0.30**	-0.58***	-0.70***
	(1.9)	(2.0)	(4.0)	(5.3)	(1.9)	(2.0)	(4.0)	(5.3)
λ (H-P)			0.34	1.11***			0.30	1.10***
			(1.5)	(4.2)			(1.2)	(3.9)
D			-0.00	1.43***			0.02	1.52***
			(0.0)	(2.6)			(0.1)	(2.7)
Share of 20–24			0.52***	0.64***			0.56***	0.70***
			(7.2)	(8.5)			(7.4)	(8.7)
Share of 15–64			0.21***	0.35***			0.21***	0.35***
			(3.8)	(4.9)			(3.7)	(4.8)
R-squared	0.03	0.04	0.32	0.45	0.60	0.60	0.74	0.79
F-statistic	7.5	2.41	26.0	22.0	313.0	78.6	157.7	101.5
Obs.	420	420	337	337	420	420	337	337
Period	1960–19	1960–19	1960 -19	1960 -19	1960–19	1960–19	1960 -19	1960 -19
Fixed effects (F)		0.73 p = 0.63		12.5 p = 0.00		0.77 p = 0.59		63.4 p = 0.00

Note: The nominal interest rate is measured by the yield on one-year government debt. t-statistics in parentheses. Equation estimated using a fixed-effect estimator. *** denotes significance at the 1% level, ** denotes significance at the 5% level, and * significance at the 10% level

by less than the increase in inflation. The inclusion of the (smoothed) rate of productivity growth and the share of government debt in GDP gives a positive, marginally significant coefficient of productivity growth but a statistically insignificant coefficient of debt. A one percentage point increase in the rate of productivity growth makes interest rates go up by 0.34%.[5] Finally, both the share of young workers and the share of the working-age population have statistically significant coefficients. The size of the two coefficients is also economically significant: a one percentage point increase in the share of the young makes real interest rates rise by 0.52%, and a one percentage point increase in the share of the working-age population makes real interest rates rise by 0.21%. In column (4), we then estimate the same equation using a fixed-effects estimator. The coefficients of inflation and unemployment rise—indicating that higher unemployment lowers the real rate more, as does higher inflation—while the coefficient of productivity growth becomes much more significant, both statistically and economically. A one percentage point increase in productivity growth raises real interest rates by 1.1%. The coefficient of debt now becomes significant with the expected sign. A ten percentage point increase in the ratio of government debt to GDP makes the real rate increase by 0.14%. Finally, the effect of the demographic variables is larger than in column (3).

In columns (5) to (9), we replace the short real rate with the short nominal rate of interest measured by the yield on one-year government bonds. The results are consistent with those in columns (1) to (4).

We can then use the estimated coefficient of productivity growth to assess the extent to which changes in productivity growth explain changes in the real rate of interest in the G7 countries. Table 5.7 shows the average rates of total factor productivity growth in the G7 countries by half-decades. The last line shows the decline over the entire period from the early 1960s to recent years.

There has been a decline from the early 1960s in all the countries. In the US and Canada, the largest decline is between the late 1960s and the early 1970s, while in Japan and the four European countries the slowdown occurs in the 1980s. The coefficient of productivity growth in column (4) of Table 5.6 is 1.11. The implied fall in the real rate of interest in France from the early 1980s to the late 2010s is then 1.11*(1.71–0.56) = 1.28%; for Italy it is 1.01%; and for the US it is (1.66–0.81)*1.11 = 0.60% since the late-1990s productivity surge and (2.12–0.81)*1.11 = 1.45%

[5] Rachel and Summers (2019) find that a slowdown in the trend TFP growth rate of 0.8 percent per year leads to a 1.8 percent decline in the real rate of interest.

Table 5.7 Average rates of total factor productivity growth (%)

	Canada	*France*	*Germany*	*Italy*	*Japan*	*UK*	*US*
1961–1965	1.95	3.76	3.49	4.32	5.04	1.96	2.12
1966–1970	1.79	3.58	3.05	4.03	4.55	2.23	1.68
1971–1975	1.04	2.88	2.76	2.82	2.82	1.77	0.98
1976–1980	0.29	2.03	2.14	1.69	1.89	1.70	0.70
1981–1985	0.12	1.71	1.72	1.15	2.09	1.84	0.88
1986–1990	0.17	1.38	1.85	1.31	1.73	1.53	1.13
1991–1995	0.68	1.19	1.86	1.22	0.41	1.61	1.39
1996–2000	1.20	1.37	1.44	0.64	-0.28	1.78	1.66
2001–2005	0.79	0.97	0.81	-0.13	0.05	1.32	1.35
2006–2010	0.19	0.20	0.47	-0.55	0.28	0.42	0.83
2011–2015	0.31	0.18	0.63	-0.26	0.41	0.21	0.70
2016–2019	0.65	0.56	0.79	0.24	0.21	0.36	0.81
Change from first period (top row) to last period (bottom row)	-1.30	-3.20	-2.70	-4.08	-4.83	-1.60	-1.31

Source Bergeaud et al. (2022)

since the early 1960s. The largest predicted fall is in Japan, where productivity growth rates fell from 2.09% in the early 1980s to 0.21% in the late 2010s, which implies a (2.09–0.21)*1.11 = 2.09% fall in real interest rates.

Figures 5.5 and 5.6 show actual short-term real and nominal rates and the rates predicted from the results in columns (4) and (8) of Table 5.6.

The estimated equations manage to capture the downward trend of the real rates and the nominal rate in the seven countries.[6] A notable discrepancy is the US in the early 1980s, when the monetary policy response was stronger than that estimated in Table 5.6. Another discrepancy is the short-lived attempts by the French and Italian central banks to defend a peg against the Deutschmark in 1992.

We have used the *ex post* real rate of interest calculated as the difference between the nominal yield on government debt and the annual change in the consumer price index. However, for investment decisions it is the *ex ante* real rate that matters. Figure 5.7 shows the ten-year *ex ante* real interest rate on US government bonds against our measure of the *ex post* real rate of interest. Clearly, the two series share a downward-sloping path from 1980 to 2019.

We conclude that using the *ex post* real interest rates in the preceding analysis should not be misleading from the 1980s on.

[6] The predicted values do not start in 1960, due to missing observations on the share of the young and the working-age population.

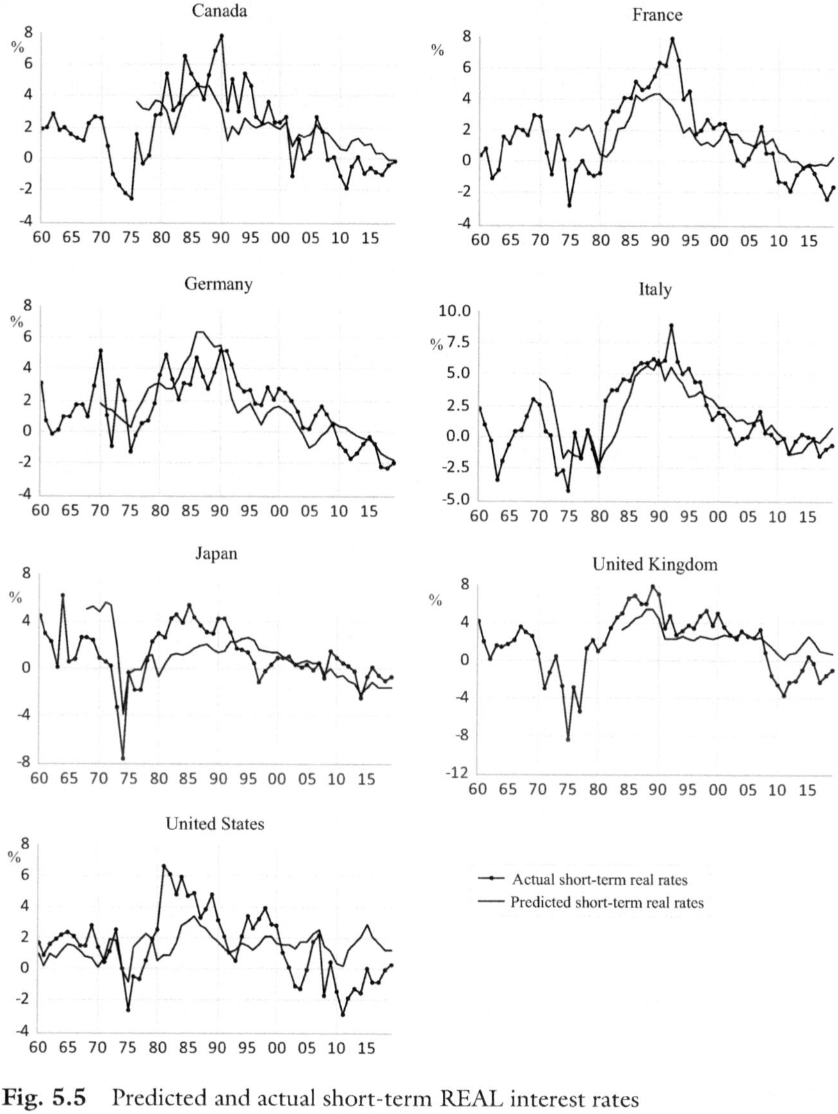

Fig. 5.5 Predicted and actual short-term REAL interest rates

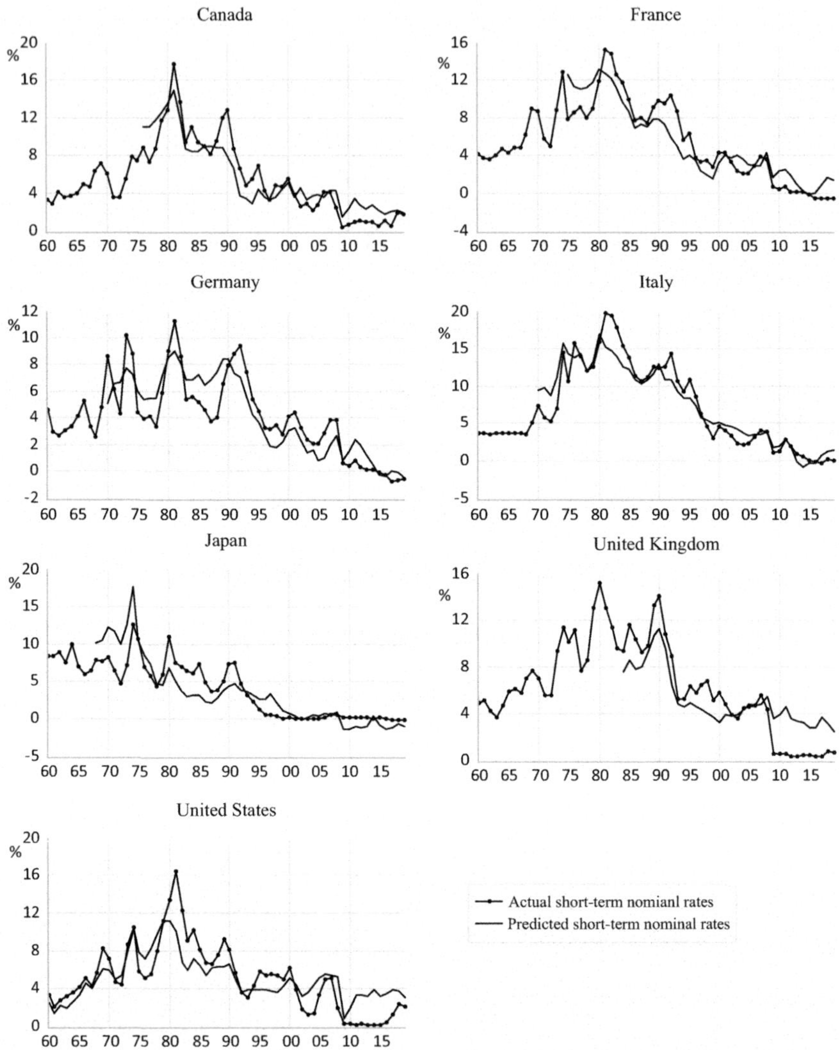

Fig. 5.6 Predicted and actual short-term NOMINAL interest rates

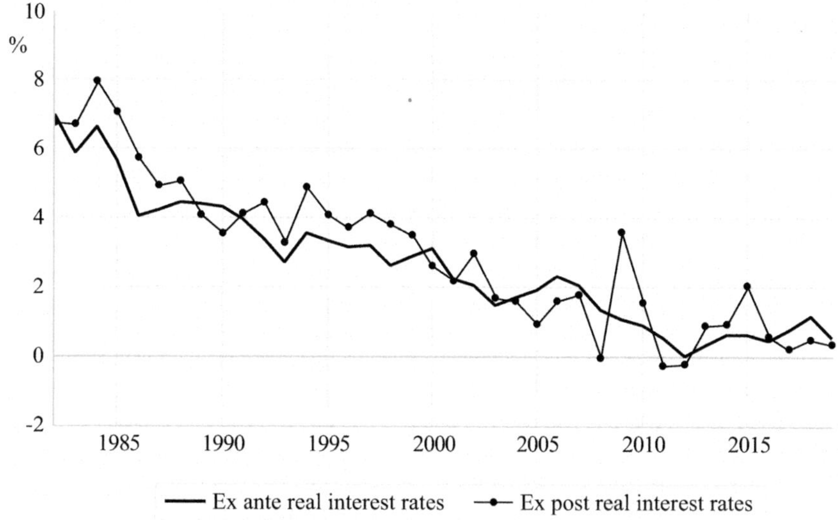

The *ex-ante* real rate is the ten-year real rate of interest on US government debt, with inflation expectations estimated by the Federal Reserve Bank of Cleveland based on the inflation risk premium, the real risk premium, and the real interest rate.

Fig. 5.7 Ex-ante and ex-post (long) interest rates. Source: Federal Reserve Bank of Cleveland (2022)

5.4 Effect on Other Variables

By using the historical database of Jorda, Schularick and Taylor (2019) and the productivity data collected by the Bank of France (see Bergeaud et al., 2022), we can estimate the relationship between causal variables in our model, such as productivity growth, population growth, and government debt, on the one hand, and the rate of return on capital, investment, real wage growth, and employment, on the other. We use the period from 1925 to 2019. The year 1925 is chosen because of the effect of WWI, as well as the hyperinflation in Germany at the beginning of the decade.[7] We end our sample in 2019 because of the effect of the COVID-19 pandemic.

[7] Inflation in Germany was 212% in 1924 but had subsided to 9.0% by 1925.

Table 5.8 Return on equity and housing

Short run: b	Δ *Risky return*	Δ *Investment*	Δ *Real wage growth*	Δ *Employment*
Δ λ	-0.01 (2.4)**	0.04 (1.9)*	-0.02 (0.5)	-0.0 (2.4)**
Δ*D*	-0.05 (1.0)	-0.01 (1.0)	0.01(0.8)	-3.26 (5.4)**
Δ*n*	-0.00 (0.5)	-0.03 (0.5)	0.01 (0.1)	0.06 (1.1)
Δ *dep (t-1)*	-0.07 (1.6)	0.16 (3.9)**	-0.06 (1.7)*	0.32 (8.9)**
Adjustment: -μ				
dep (t-1)	-0.66 (12.6)**	-0.06 (4.2)**	-0.06 (1.7)*	-0.11 (8.3)**
Long run: θ				
λ	0.02 (4.2)**	1.78 (4.4)**	0.41 (5.1)**	0.13 (7.4)**
D	-0.06 (1.4)	-0.11 (1.3)	-0.04 (3.9)**	0.51 (2.3)**
D^2	0.01 (0.7)	0.00 (1.3)	0.00 (3.2)**	-0.14 (1.6)
n	-0.00 (0.3)	0.09 (1.8)*	0.08 (0.9)	-0.06 (1.5)
Observations	456	629	620	601
Years	1926–2019	1926–2019	1928–2019	1927–2019
R-squared	0.37	0.17	0.33	0.35
F	18.4	8.25	19.7	20.6

Note: Estimation method: Least squares with fixed effects, *t*-statistics in parentheses. Significance at the 5% level denoted by ** and significance at the 10% level by *

We use dynamic models, which explain the change in a dependent variable by its lagged change and a set of explanatory variables. The following is the fixed-effects estimator, which has heterogeneous intercepts but homogeneous short-run and long-run coefficients:

$$\Delta y_{it} = c_i + \boldsymbol{b}'\Delta x_{i,t} - \mu\left(y_{i,t-1} - \theta' x_{i,t-1}\right) + \delta \Delta y_{i,t-1} + u_{i,t}, \tag{5.4}$$

where x is a vector of regressors and y is the dependent variable. The estimator is robust to the order of integration or cointegration of the variables.

The vector y has the rate of return on capital (housing and stocks), the investment-to-output ratio, real wage growth, and employment (100 minus the rate of unemployment). The vector x has a set of explanatory variables: productivity growth, population growth (average of lagged terms 19, 20, and 21 years ago), and public debt as a share of output as regressors (Table 5.8). We include a squared value of the debt-to-output ratio to capture the nonlinearity in the relationship between debt, the stock of capital, and the real rate of interest as shown in Chap. 2.[8]

The results show that the rate of productivity growth has a positive long-run effect on the rate of return on housing and stocks, investment, labor force participation, and the employment rate. Public debt has a negative effect on the return on risky assets in the long run, as well as on investment and real wage growth, but surprisingly, it has a positive effect on employment, perhaps due to a Keynesian wealth effect.[9] The effect of lagged population growth is weak.

In the short run, however, an increase in the rate of productivity growth has the effect of lowering the return on risky assets, increasing investment, and reducing employment, while an increase in public debt also lowers employment.

5.5 Share Prices and Markups

The models in Chaps. 3 and 4 describe how falling rates of productivity growth have the effect of raising the shadow price of capital in a two-sector model and increasing the markup of price over marginal cost in a two-sector model with customer markets in the consumer-goods sector.

[8] Reinhart and Rogoff (2010) estimated a debt-to-GDP threshold above which a further increase in debt has adverse effects on the rate of growth of output. However, Chudik et al. (2017) found no such threshold using a sample of 40 countries over the period 1965 to 2010.

[9] Gale and Orszag reviewed the literature on the relationship between government deficits and interest rates and concluded that the effect of government deficits on real rates is positive and economically significant—that a one percent increase in the deficit-to-GDP ratio tends to raise interest rates by around 50–100 basis points. More recent studies confirm these results. Engen and Hubbard (2004) found a positive effect of debt on interest rates: a one per cent rise in government debt as a ratio to GDP raises interest rates by about three basis points. Laubach (2009) found that a rise in government deficits of one per cent of GDP raises interest rates by about 20–30 basis points and that an equal increase in the debt-to-GDP ratio results in a rise of about 3–4 basis points. Smith (2022) examined the effect of the stock of public debt, government deficits, and changes in the public debt-to-GDP ratio on long (ten-year) interest rates in a panel of 17 countries from 1870 to 2016. He found that it is the change in debt, rather than the debt level or the deficit, that matters for long interest rates.

A fall in the rate of productivity growth lowers the stock of human capital, which raises the supply of wealth and lowers the equilibrium real rate of interest as derived in Chap. 2. A fall in population growth has a similar effect by making the supply of wealth increase. As the real interest rate declines, the shadow price of a unit of physical capital increases as shown in Chap. 3. In the data, we can use share prices to proxy for the shadow price of capital. We normalize the share price index by the level of TFP productivity because share prices, as well as wages, grow at the rate of productivity growth in equilibrium.[10]

In Chap. 4, we saw that the fall in the rate of productivity growth also affected the markups, that is, the ratio of price to marginal cost. The fall in productivity growth lowers the normalized value of customers through a discounting effect, which raises markups, as firms value their market share less and choose to increase current profits in the expectation that their future market share will be reduced. In symmetric equilibrium, market shares are unchanged but markups are higher. The higher markups are, the lower the rental of capital, which reduces nonhuman wealth, and in turn lowers consumption and raises the supply of wealth, further reducing the real rate of interest. A fall in population growth also has the effect of raising markups. The effect goes through a lower value of the shadow price of customers normalized by productivity, market share being less valuable when the population is expected to increase at a slower rate. This reduces the return on customers—in particular, the capital gain on expanding the customer base. To put it simply, having a larger market share is less valuable when the size of the market is expected to grow more slowly than before, and markups are therefore higher.

Figure 5.8 shows two time series for the US and Germany. The top figure has average markups for Europe and normalized share prices for Germany, the largest European country. The bottom figure has markups for North America and normalized share prices for the US.

The two series move together in both figures. Markups and share prices rise in the 1980s and again in recent years. Also note the financial booms in the late 1990s and in the first decade of this century, which made share prices rise and then fall in both countries. Both booms saw a small but significant rise in markups.

[10] Strictly speaking, this should be the productivity of capital in the production of the consumer good.

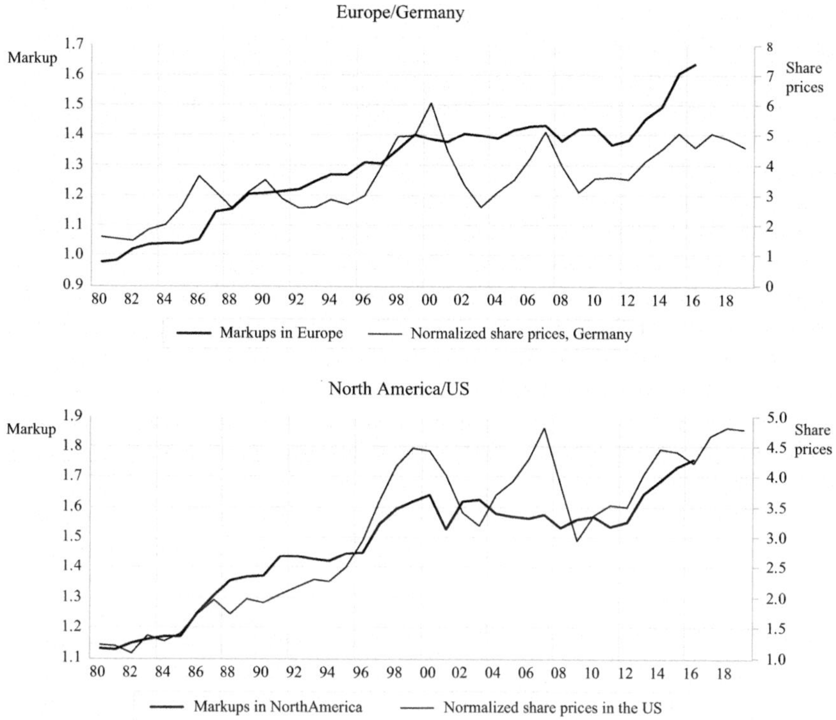

Fig. 5.8 Markups and share prices normalized by productivity. Source: Eeckhout (2022a, 2022b) and OECD

5.6 Job Satisfaction

While productivity growth and rising wages may yield greater job satisfaction, more satisfied workers also tend to be more productive.[11] One possible consequence of the economic stagnation caused by lower rates of productivity growth is a loss of job satisfaction. In Chap. 2, we showed how a reduction in job satisfaction may be modeled as an increase in the disutility of work. This would raise the ratio of the real wage to nonwage income and reduce the supply of labor by each working individual.

[11] See Oswald et al. (2015), amongst others.

The study of life and job satisfaction has a long history in economics. Freeman (1978) was one of the first studies in the economics of job satisfaction. He found, unsurprisingly, that the level of job satisfaction is a significant determinant of the probability of quitting. Blanchflower and Oswald (2004) studied reported happiness in the US and UK using the *General Social Survey* for the US and the *Eurobarometer Survey* for the UK. They found that the proportion of respondents who claim to be "very happy" fell from 34% in the early 1970s to 30% in the late 1990s. The downward trend is explained by the decline in the share of women who report being very happy, from 36% at the start of the period to 29% in the late 1990s. In contrast, using a life-satisfaction question from the *Eurobarometer Surveys* for the UK, these authors find that life satisfaction in the UK was flat from 1973 to 1998. Moreover, they found that work and family status have a strong impact on happiness and life satisfaction. Therefore, being unemployed is almost as bad as being separated or widowed.

Blanchflower and Oswald (1999) use data from the US *General Social Survey* for both men and women to document how job satisfaction in the US had been slowly trending downwards. They find that job satisfaction is greater among older workers, women, the self-employed, and whites. Their explanation for falling levels of job satisfaction is mainly that workers have increasingly come to fear for their jobs. Workers who answer that they are not at all likely to lose their job report greater job satisfaction. In addition, people who say that it would be easy to find another job report higher levels of job satisfaction. Moreover, and unsurprisingly, higher wages increase job satisfaction. What did come as a surprise was that education does not contribute to job satisfaction.

Hamermesh (2001) used *the National Longitudinal Survey* cohort of young men (NLSYM) and found a widening of the distribution of job satisfaction across cohorts of young men in the US between the late 1970s and the mid-1990s that correlated with changing wage inequality. Thus job satisfaction among workers in the top earnings quantiles increased compared to that of workers in lower quantiles. He attributed the low levels of satisfaction in the latter group to workers' disappointment about their wages.

Francis Green (2005) used indicators of job satisfaction taken from public opinion surveys and administrative data. He found that average pay levels had increased in most developed countries apart from the US. Also, skill requirements had increased, which could be expected to generate more job satisfaction. But contrary to expectations, he found greater inequality, increased required work effort, diminished job satisfaction, and a loss of worker autonomy on the job. He attributed the changes in the quality of work life to technological change and transformations in the political-economic environment.

There is some emerging evidence of worker distress. In a more recent paper, Blanchflower and Oswald (2020) study the evolution of "extreme distress" in the US from 1993 to 2019 using the *Behavioral Risk Factor Surveillance System*, which collects state-level data about US residents with the assistance of the *Centers for Disease Control and Prevention*. An individual is classified as being extremely distressed if, in response to the question, "Now thinking about your mental health, which includes stress, depression, and problems with emotions, for how many days during the past 30 days was your mental health not good?" they say that their mental health was not good for all 30 days. Thus, for the extremely distressed, every day was a bad day. Blanchflower and Oswald find that the proportion of the US population in extreme distress rose from 3.6% in 1993 to 6.4% in 2019. This upward trend masks a much steeper increase among the noncollege educated, middle-aged white population, for whom the proportion reporting extreme distress rose from 5% in 1993 to 11% in 2019.

5.7 Summary

Interest rates have fallen in the past four decades in the G7 countries. The fall is apparent in each of the interest rate series as well as found to have a significant shared component. Using a panel estimation of an expanded Taylor equation, we have found that the productivity growth slowdown can account for the fall in the real interest rate. Moreover, the productivity slowdown contributes to explaining the fall in the rate of return to equity and housing, the fall in investment, the fall in real wage growth and falling employment. Rising share prices are shown to go together with rising markups for the US and Canada and for Europe. Finally, we have surveyed a literature that shows rising rates of job dissatisfaction and increased worker distress in the West.

References

Bergeaud, A., Cette, G., & Lecat, R. (2022, November 24). *The long-term productivity database*. Prod. Bank of France.http://www.longtermproductivity.com/about.html.

Blanchflower, D. G., & Oswald, A. J. (1999). *Well-being, insecurity and the decline of American job satisfaction*. Manuscript. Unpublished manuscript. https://www.researchgate.net/profile/Andrew-Oswald/publication/2548976_Well-Being_Insecurity_and_the_Decline_of_American_Job_Satisfaction/links/5591133708ae15962d8c7a4a/Well-Being-Insecurity-and-the-Decline-of-American-Job-Satisfaction.pdf.

Blanchflower, D. G., & Oswald, A. J. (2004). Well-being over time in Britain and the USA. *Journal of Public Economics, 88*(7–8), 1359–1386.

Blanchflower, D. G., & Oswald, A. J. (2020). Trend in extreme distress in the United States, 1993-2019. *American Journal of Public Health, 110*(10), 1538–1544.

Christiano, L., Eichenbaum, M., & Evans, C. (1996). The effects of monetary policy shocks: Evidence from the flow of funds. *Review of Economics and Statistics, 78*, 16–34.

Chudik, A., Mohaddes, K., Pesaran, M. H., & Raissi, M. (2017). Is there a debt threshold effect on output growth?. *Review of Economics and Statistics, 99*(1), 135–50.

Del Negro, M., Giannone, D., Giannoni, M. P., & Tambalotti, A. (2019). Global trends in interest rates. *Journal of International Economics, 118*, 248–262.

Eeckhout, J. (2022a, October 31). *The profit paradox: How thriving firms threaten the future of work*. https://www.theprofitparadox.com/

Eeckhout, J. (2022b). *The profit paradox: How thriving firms threaten the future of work*. Princeton, NJ: Princeton University Press.

Engen, E. M., & Hubbard, R. G. (2004). Federal government debt and interst rates. *NBER Macroeconomics Annual, 19*, 83–138.

Federal Reserve Bank of Cleveland. (2022). *10-year real interest rate (REAINTRATREARAT10Y). Statistics*. FRED, Federal Reserve Bank of St. Louis. Accessed August 11, 2022, from https://fred.stlouisfed.org/series/REAINTRATREARAT10Y

Freeman, R. B. (1978). Job satisfaction as an economic variable. *American Economic Review, 68*(2), 135–141.

Green, F. (2005). *Demanding work: The paradox of job quality in the affluent economy*. Princeton, NJ: Princeton University Press.

Hamermesh, D. S. (2001). The changing distribution of job satisfaction. *Journal of Human Resources, 36*(1), 1–30.

Jorda, O., Knoll, E., Kuvshinov, M., Schularick, M., & Taylor, A. M. (2019). The rate of return on everything, 1870-2015. *Quarterly Journal of Economics, 134*(3), 1225–1298.

Laubach, T. (2009). New evidence on the interest rate effects of budget deficits and debt. *Journal of the European Economic Association, 7*(4), 858–885.

Onatski, A., & Wang, C. (2021). Spurious factor analysis. *Econometrica, 89*(2), 591–614.

Oswald, A. J., Proto, E., & Sgroi, D. (2015). Happiness and productivity. *Journal of Labor Economics, 33*(4), 789–822.

Rachel, L., & Summers, L. H. (2019). *On Secular stagnation in the industrialized world*. NBER Working Paper 26198.

Reinhart, C. M., & Rogoff, K. S. (2010). Growth in a time of debt. *American Economic Review, 100*, 573–578.

Smith, R. (2022). Government debt, deficits and interst rates 1870–2016. *Essays in honor of M. Hashem Pesaran: Prediction and macro modeling, 43A*, 323–340.

CHAPTER 6

Losing Ground

In this chapter, we analyze the relationship between a technology leader and a follower. We have China and the US in mind from recent times, the US being the technology leader. In past decades, the role of China was played by Japan, South Korea, Taiwan, Singapore, and other countries in Asia and Western Europe in the postwar decades.

We pay attention to three developments in this chapter. The first is that the follower country learns from the US, as in Nelson and Phelps (1966), and gradually closes the technology gap. The second element of our study is that the US stagnates, which also leaves a smaller equilibrium technology gap with follower countries. Third, in the case of China, the effective labor units grow faster than those in the US due to catch-up growth, and China becomes an even larger part of the world economy. Thus we explore a world where a leading country gradually loses both its own dynamism and its productivity advantage over an emerging rival, while the latter becomes a larger part of the world economy. This development explains some of the geopolitical tensions we have in the world.

In addition, we explore the implications of rising public debt in the US in recent decades in a two-country setting. In our finite-life and unconnected families framework, public debt is an asset for individuals but not

E. Phelps et al., *The Great Economic Slowdown*,
https://doi.org/10.1007/978-3-031-31441-4_6

for the economy as a whole, and the rise of public debt in the leading economy has implications for both countries, as we will show.[1]

Finally, we expand our analysis to cover the G7 countries. The catch-up growth in Western Europe in the decades following WWII and a similar episode in Japan resembled China's recent growth surge. The slowdown in productivity growth in Japan and Europe in recent decades also resembles the current slowdown in China.

6.1 One-Country Model with a Public Sector

We start by reviewing a one-country model similar to that in Chap. 2 before deriving a two-country model.

The model has finite horizons in both countries, which generates debt non-neutrality. The two economies are connected through an integrated capital market. The two countries trade in bonds due to differences in saving and the intertemporal allocation of consumption. The countries differ in their rate of population growth as well as the rate of pure time preference. In today's world economy, we think of China as having the lower rate of time preference, which generates a lower level of consumption and a lower autarkic real interest rate. When the capital markets of the countries with high and low rates of time preference—the US and China—are integrated, the real rate of interest rises in China and falls in the US when capital flows from the former to the latter. We now turn to the elements of the model.[2]

[1] The relationship between fiscal policy in the US and unemployment in Europe in the 1980s can be explained in this setting if a wage curve is added to the model. Higher world interest rates have the effect of raising markups in the model in Chap. 4, which is equivalent to a fall in the real demand wage. With real wage rigidity—which is not in the model in Chap. 4—unemployment rises. (See Fitoussi and Phelps (1986), Fitoussi and Phelps (1988), Phelps (1994) and Fitoussi et al. (2000).) A model where real interest rates raise unemployment by lowering investment in new employees is derived by Hoon and Phelps (1992). Phelps (1999) explains the 1990s employment boom in the US by a rise in productivity growth in a non-monetary setting.

[2] Buiter (1981) uses a two-period overlapping-generations model to study the effect of differences in the rate of time preference between two countries on capital movements. In his model, capital flows from a country with a lower rate of time preference to a country with a higher rate of time preference when the working generation in the country with a lower rate lends money to the country with the higher rate. Kikuchi and Hamada (2011) extend the Buiter model by introducing a labor-intensive nontradable sector. Hamada et al. (2009), in an unpublished paper, extend the analysis to the perpetual youth model of Blanchard (1985).

Population and Technology

There is a growing population in both countries and the size of the population is equal to the size of the labor force. We set the size of the population equal to $N_0 e^{nt}$. By assumption, the supply of labor per worker is fixed and equal to $\overline{L}$. Technology is labor-augmenting and technical progress is equal to λ, so that $\Lambda_t = \Lambda_0 e^{\lambda t}$. The number of effective units of labor is then $N_0 e^{\lambda t} \overline{L}$, where N denotes the number of workers.

Consumption

There are overlapping generations, each enjoying perpetual youth (as in Blanchard, 1985) with a constant probability of death given by θ. New cohorts are not linked to current dynasties through operative bequests and enter the economy as in Buiter (1988) and Weil (1989). With a subjective rate of time preference, ρ, and the log period utility function, the per capita aggregate consumption function is given by

$$C = (\theta + \rho)(H + W), \tag{6.1}$$

where C is per capita aggregate consumption, H is human wealth, and W is per capita aggregate nonhuman wealth, which evolves according to

$$\dot{W} = (r - n)W + v - T - C, \tag{6.2}$$

v being the real wage, r the real rate of interest, and T the lump-sum tax. H, the per capita stock of human wealth, evolves according to

$$\dot{H} = (r + \theta)H - (v - T). \tag{6.3}$$

Differentiating Eq. (6.1) with respect to time and using Eqs. (6.2) and (6.3), growth of per capita aggregate consumption is given by the Euler equation

$$\frac{\dot{C}}{C} = r - \rho - (n + \theta)(\rho + \theta)\frac{W}{C}. \tag{6.4}$$

From Eq. (6.4), it follows that an unanticipated increase in the real rate r makes consumption drop and then rise at a faster rate. Similarly, a sudden increase in the rate of time preference ρ would make consumption jump and then increase at a less rapid rate.

Production

Production involves the neoclassical one-good production function under perfect competition, with output $Z = F\left(K, \Lambda N\bar{L}\right) = \Lambda N f\left(\tilde{k}\right)$, where $\tilde{k} \equiv K / \left(\Lambda N\bar{L}\right)$ is physical capital per effective worker. Profit maximization yields

$$\tilde{v} = f\left(\tilde{k}\right) - \tilde{k} f'\left(\tilde{k}\right), \tag{6.5}$$

$$r = f'\left(\tilde{k}\right) - \delta, \tag{6.6}$$

where $\tilde{v} \equiv v / \Lambda$ is the real wage per effective worker and δ is the depreciation rate of capital. Eqs. (6.5) and (6.6) together give the factor-price frontier, $\tilde{v} = \phi\left(r\right); \phi'(r) < 0$.

Equilibrium

The equilibrium real rate of interest and the equilibrium stock of capital occur at the intersection of the demand-for-capital curve and the supply-of-wealth curve. Using Eq. (6.6), we find that $\tilde{K} \equiv \dfrac{K}{\Lambda N} = f'^{-1}\left(r\right)\bar{L}$, as is shown by the downward-sloping curve on the right-hand side of Fig. 6.1.

Turning to the supply-of-wealth curve, in steady state, Eqs. (6.1), (6.3), and (6.4) give

$$r = \rho + \lambda + \left(n + \theta\right)\left[\frac{\tilde{W}}{\tilde{H} + \tilde{W}}\right], \tag{6.7}$$

where $\tilde{W} \equiv W / \Lambda$, $\tilde{H} \equiv H / \Lambda = \left[\phi\left(r\right) - \tilde{T}\right] / \left[r - \lambda - \theta\right]$ and $\tilde{T}$ is a lump-sum tax per effective worker. If the stock of human wealth is not too sensitive to the real interest rate, r, then we can obtain an upward-sloping curve on the right-hand side of Fig. 6.1.[3]

[3] The condition is given by $0 < -\left[\left(n+\theta\right)\tilde{W} / \left(\tilde{H} + \tilde{W}\right)^2\right]\left\{\left[\phi'(r) - \tilde{H}\right] / \left[r - \lambda + \theta\right]\right\} < 1$.

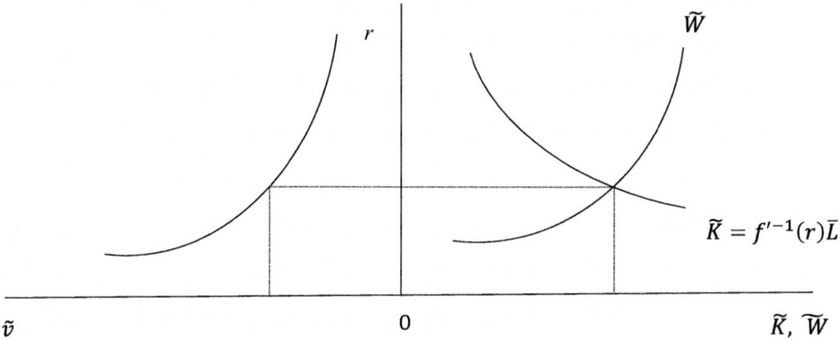

Fig. 6.1 Wages, capital, and the real rate of interest

The intersection of the two curves gives the equilibrium real rate and the equilibrium capital stock. The left-hand panel then shows the factor-price frontier, which gives the equilibrium real wage per effective worker $\tilde{v} \equiv v / \Lambda$.

Government

We assume that the government does not buy anything from the private sector and that government purchases are equal to zero. Instead, the government only services its debt by taxing the private sector with the lump-sum tax $\tilde{T}$

$$\dot{\tilde{D}} = -\tilde{T} + \left[r - (n + \lambda)\right]\tilde{D}, \tag{6.8}$$

where $\tilde{D}$ is the stock of public debt per effective worker and $\tilde{T}$ is taxes per effective worker.

6.2 Two-Country Model With a Public Sector

Let there be two countries: Country 1 (the US, the technology leader) and Country 2 (China, the technology follower)—where each is as described in Sect. 6.1. We now introduce capital flows between the two countries. In such a two-country world, the world rate of interest will be between the autarkic interest rates in the two countries. One of the countries will turn out to be a net debtor country and the other a net creditor country.

The following system of equations summarizes the global equilibrium under the assumption of perfect international capital mobility:

$$r = \rho_1 + \lambda_1 + (n_1 + \theta_1)\left|\frac{\tilde{W}_1}{\tilde{H}_1 + \tilde{W}_1}\right|, \tag{6.9}$$

$$r = \rho_2 + \lambda_2 + (n_2 + \theta_2)\left|\frac{\tilde{W}_2}{\tilde{H}_2 + \tilde{W}_2}\right|, \tag{6.10}$$

where $\tilde{W}_1 \equiv W_1 / \Lambda_1 \equiv \tilde{K}_1 + \tilde{D}_1 + \tilde{F}_1$, $\tilde{D}$ is normalized public debt, and $\tilde{F}$ is normalized net foreign assets, and

$$\tilde{W}_2 \equiv W_2 / \Lambda_2 \equiv \tilde{K}_2 + \tilde{D}_2 - (\Lambda_1 / \Lambda_2)\tilde{F}_1, \tilde{K} = f'^{-1}(r)\bar{L}.$$

We allow the two countries to differ in terms of the rate of time preference, the rate of productivity growth, population growth, and life expectancy, but to share a capital market, making them face the same real rate of interest r. From Eq. (6.3) it follows that, in steady state, the normalized (by technology) steady-state stock of human capital is

$$\tilde{H}_1 = \frac{\phi(r) - \tilde{T}_1}{r - \lambda_1 + \theta_1}, \tag{6.11}$$

$$\tilde{H}_2 = \frac{\phi(r) - \tilde{T}_2}{r - \lambda_2 + \theta_2}, \tag{6.12}$$

with $\tilde{T}_1 = [r - (n_1 + \lambda_1)]\tilde{D}_1$ and $\tilde{T}_2 = [r - (n_2 + \lambda_2)]\tilde{D}_2$. Hence, given $\tilde{D}_1$ and $\tilde{D}_2$, Eqs. (6.9) and (6.10) solve for world real interest rates, r, and the stock of net foreign assets per effective worker in Country 1.[4]

In Fig. 6.2, Case I depicts a scenario with $\tilde{D}_1 = 0$ and $\tilde{D}_2 = 0$. Parameter values are such that the autarkic interest rate is higher in Country 1 than in Country 2, due to a lower rate of time preference ρ in Country 2. With free international capital mobility, there are capital inflows into Country 1, which becomes the international net debtor. The presence of $\tilde{F}_1 < 0$ drives a wedge in both the left-hand and the right-hand diagrams. The equilibrium world real interest rate is given by r^*. Compared to autarky, there is

[4] In a two-country world, $F_2 = - F_1$, which, when normalized by national productivity levels, can be written as $\tilde{F}_2 = -(\Lambda_1 / \Lambda_2)\tilde{F}_1$.

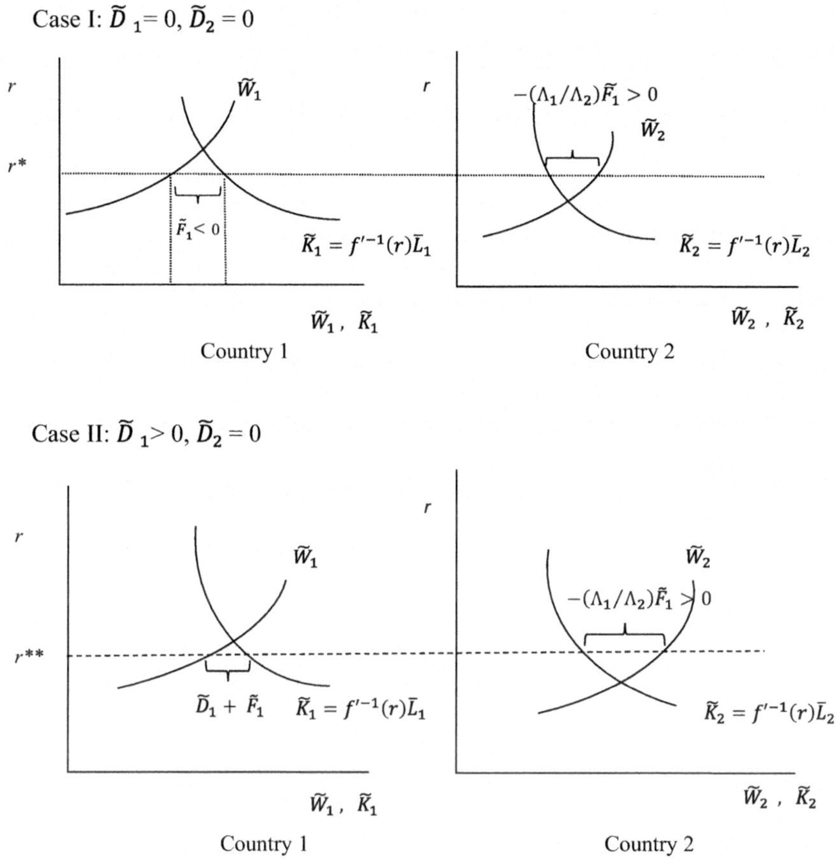

Fig. 6.2 The effect of debt in a two-country model

more capital in the net debtor country and less in the creditor country. The capital flows reduce net wealth in the debtor country but increase it in the creditor country. In essence, the creditor country has extended its ownership of capital located in its own country through the bond market to include capital located in the debtor country. With more capital situated in the debtor country, real wages are higher than in autarky, while the real wage in the creditor country falls. The increased foreign debt in the debtor country in the new steady states requires the creditor country to run a permanent trade surplus to service its increased debt.

We now introduce public debt in Country 1, which is the debtor country. In Fig. 6.2, Case II depicts a scenario with $\tilde{D}_1 > 0$ and $\tilde{D}_2 = 0$. In response to the debt accumulation, capital flows from Country 2 into Country 1, driving the world real interest rate, r^*, higher than in Case I and reducing the stock of capital in both countries. When Country 1 increases its level of public debt, the effect is to increase household wealth in that country, which raises consumption and the equilibrium real rate of interest. This causes a further capital flow from the creditor country to Country 1, and the world real interest rate rises. The net effect is to lower the stock of capital in both countries and to make Country 1 more indebted to Country 2 while, paradoxically, making households in Country 1 feel wealthier due to the failure of Ricardian equivalence in the Blanchard-Buiter-Weil framework.

The two countries correspond to the US being a debtor country since the early 1980s and China becoming a large creditor country. The reader may observe that the US still has a current account deficit or a capital account surplus, which in the light of the model suggests that the two countries have still not reached a steady state.

We have assumed that the rate of time preference is lower in China, $\rho_1 > \rho_2$, which explains why the autarkic real interest rate is lower in China, and why opening up capital markets makes the real rate fall in the US and rise in China. A lower rate of population growth in China, $n_1 > n_2$, has a similar effect according to Eq. (6.7). It follows that those countries with low rates of population growth become net creditors, and countries with faster population growth become net debtors.[5]

Next we describe the flow of ideas or technology between the countries. While in stationary equilibrium, the rate of growth of technology must be the same in both countries, $\lambda_1 = \lambda_2$, the rates can differ in the transition to the equilibrium. In this context, the US—that is, Country 1—is the technology leader and China the follower, in the sense that technology in the US exceeds that in China. Country 1 (the US) is the

[5] The rate of population growth in China was 0.22% in 2020 and fell to 0% in 2021. The population growth rate in the US was 0.4% in 2020 and 0.3% in 2021. China's population is projected to decline for the rest of this century, while the population of the US is expected to rise. See www.macrotrends.net

technology leader, $\Lambda_1(t) > \Lambda_2(t)$, while Country 2 (China) learns from the leader. Following Nelson and Phelps (1966), suppose that we write

$$\frac{d\Lambda_2(t)}{dt} = \kappa\left[\Lambda_1(t) - \Lambda_2(t)\right]; \kappa > 0, \tag{6.13}$$

so the rate at which the frontier technology (represented by Λ_1) is realized in improved technological practice in Country 2, which depends positively on the gap between frontier technology and the technology in the follower country, in addition to the ability to learn, κ. The ability to learn may increase through higher education and foreign direct investment, to take two examples.[6]

Dividing both sides of Eq. (6.13) by Λ_2, we obtain

$$\lambda_2(t) = \kappa\left[\frac{\Lambda_1(t)}{\Lambda_2(t)} - 1\right]. \tag{6.14}$$

In steady state, the technology in practice in Country 2 grows at the exogenously given rate of frontier technology in Country 1—that is, $\lambda_2 = \lambda_1$—so we can write the technology gap Λ_1/Λ_2 in equilibrium as a positive function of the rate of productivity growth in the leading country λ_1 and a negative function of the follower country's ability to learn and adopt the leader's technology:

$$\frac{\Lambda_1}{\Lambda_2} = \frac{\lambda_1}{\kappa} + 1. \tag{6.15}$$

[6] Vandenbussche et al. (2006) examine the contribution of human capital to technological growth through innovation and imitation. Their theoretical model shows that skilled labor is more important when an economy finds itself close to the technological frontier—Λ_1 in our notation. Their empirical results suggest that the closer an economy is to the frontier, the more important tertiary education will be for growth. In an earlier paper, Benhabib and Spiegel (1994) ran growth accounting regressions with a Cobb-Douglas production function and found that the growth rate of total factor productivity depends on the level of a nation's human capital. They make human capital affect both the rate of endogenous growth of technology and the rate of catching up to the technology leader. Ahsan and Haque (2017) use a dynamic panel threshold model and find that the positive impact of human capital on growth may not occur unless an economy is above a threshold level of development.

Hence we find that the equilibrium technology gap (Λ_1/Λ_2) narrows when the rate of technological progress in Country 1 (λ_1) declines, as we have found in the US after the early 1970s.

The technology convergence does not affect the levels of $\tilde{k}$ and $\tilde{W}$ in the two-country model with integrated capital markets. However, it does affect the level of capital and wealth per capita in both countries, as well as consumption per capita. In effect, the productivity catch-up in Country 2 makes its economy larger relative to that of Country 1, measured in effective labor units and aggregate output.[7]

6.3 The Growth of China

Several empirical implications follow from our theory. The level of productivity in other G7 countries than the US and, most importantly, in China may have converged to the US productivity level over time. This follows directly from the Nelson-Phelps model in Eq. (6.13). We begin with China.

For a fixed ability to learn, κ, the rate of growth of productivity in China should have been higher than in the US since China opened to the rest of the world in the 1990s and then gradually slowed down. But the ability to learn may also have increased, which would enable China to enjoy faster productivity growth even when the productivity gap with the US has shrunk for a multitude of reasons. The increased ability to learn can be explained by the millions of Chinese students who have studied at Western universities and then returned home as well as the significant foreign investment by Western firms in China, which involves the transfer of technology. In addition, there are the suspected espionage activities in the West by Chinese firms and government.

Second, when the rate of productivity growth in the US falls, the equilibrium gap between the US and Chinese productivity levels narrows. Thus a fall in productivity growth in the US, λ_1 in the Nelson-Phelps

[7] Our model does not capture some of the problems associated with capital market integration. There are effects working through immigration, trade, and capital flows; see Rodrik (2021). Funke et al. (2016) document the political shocks that followed financial crises in twenty developed countries after 1870 and found that financial crises increased the popularity of far-right parties. Moreover, they found that far-left parties did not experience a similar increase in their popularity and that the results are statistically stronger for the post-World War II period. In contrast, recessions that do not involve financial crises do not increase the popularity of right-wing parties.

model, has the same effect on the equilibrium productivity gap *log* (Λ_1/Λ_2) as the increase in China's ability to learn from the US, measured by κ.

Third, the Chinese economy may rival the US economy in the aggregate even when its productivity level Λ_2 remains far below the US level because of its population size. China does not need to close the productivity gap Λ_1/Λ_2 with the US to rival its hegemonic power.

Fourth, the fall in productivity growth in the US, measured by λ_1, and the higher rate of productivity growth in China, λ_2, in the transition to an equilibrium have the effect of making the effective labor force in China continue to grow relative to the effective labor force in the US.

We now illustrate each of these empirical implications. We start with the Nelson-Phelps relationship, linking productivity growth in China to the gap between the two countries. Figure 6.3 shows the rate of growth of total factor productivity in China as a function of the difference between the levels of productivity in China and the US, Λ_2/Λ_1, since 2000. There is a downward-sloping relationship so that the smaller the difference between TFP in China and the US, the lower is the rate of growth of TFP.

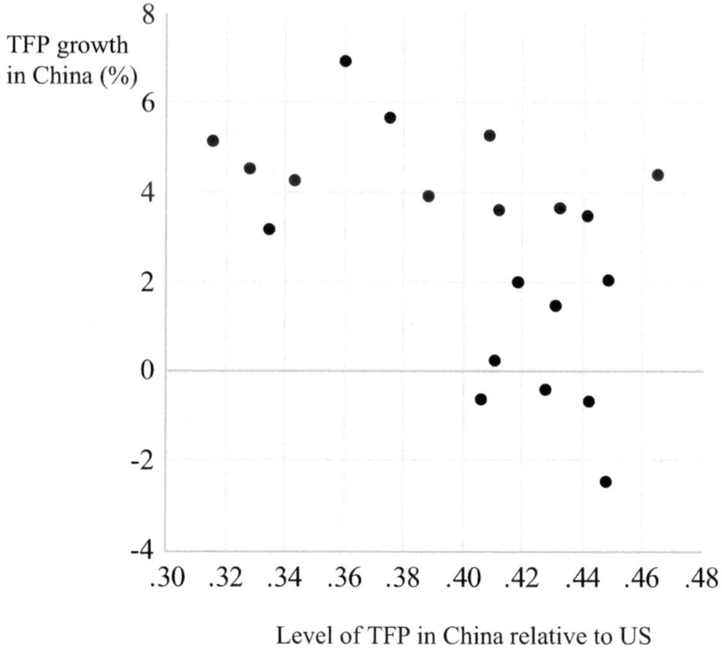

Fig. 6.3 Nelson-Phelps relationship for China, 2000–2019. Source: Penn World Tables and Bergeaud et al. (2022)

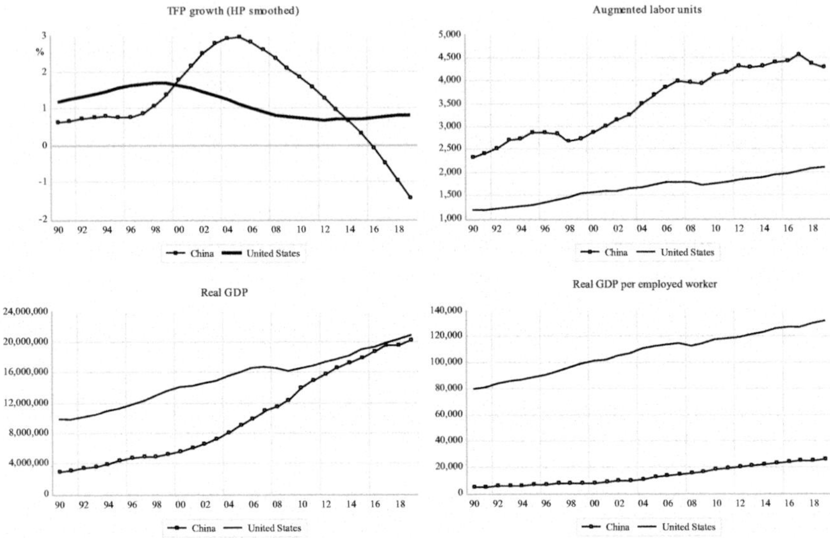

Fig. 6.4 TFP growth and augmented labor units in China and the US. Source: Penn World Tables and OECD database

The growth rate has fallen more rapidly in China after 2006 and is currently lower than the growth rate in the US. But by having more rapid productivity growth since the early 1990s, China has increased its lead in terms of the number of efficiency units of labor—the product of the level of productivity and the labor force, shown in Fig. 6.4. The rapid rise of China's augmented labor force then makes aggregate GDP in China approach the level in the US, even though its GDP per employed worker is still considerably behind that in the US.

The productivity surge in China and the catching up of Chinese GDP to the US level is an important factor behind the geopolitical rivalry between the two countries. Therefore, a resurgence of productivity growth in the US would help stymie the rivalry by placing the US firmly ahead of China in terms of the size of the economy.

There remains the effect of increased public debt in the US in this two-country equilibrium. As shown in the model of Fig. 6.2, the increased debt would raise world real interest rates and cause a fall in the stock of capital and hence real wages in the rest of the world. But this mitigates the effect of US debt on its own capital stock and real wages. Thus, contrary to the prevailing wisdom, opening up to China in terms of capital market integration shields the US worker from the effect of its own prodigal government, while allowing China to own a larger part of the US economy. In previous decades, the 1970s and the 1980s, the role of China was played by Japan and Germany, making the US change from a net creditor to a net debtor country in early 1980s. We now turn to these other countries.

6.4 THE GROWTH OF OTHERS

The rise of China is only the latest example of a country growing by adopting the technology of a leading economy. In the decades after World War II, the countries that had suffered capital destruction during the war experienced rapid growth of productivity. Table 6.1 shows average total factor productivity growth for the six G7 countries that are following the US, dating back to the 1930s.

Growth in total factor productivity took off in all six countries after the war. The productivity rebound was strongest on the European continent and in Japan, the countries that had suffered most during the war.

In comparison, we show the average productivity growth rates in the 1930s. Productivity growth was stronger in Germany and Japan than in France, Italy, and the UK in the 1930s. Following the destruction in the war, productivity growth took off in the 1950s and remained strong in the 1960s before slowing down in the 1970s and even more in the 1980s.

Table 6.1 Average TFP growth by decade (%)

	Canada	*France*	*Germany*	*Italy*	*Japan*	*UK*
1930–39	-0.5	0.2	3.0	0.2	2.1	0.2
1950–59	2.3	4.4	5.1	4.4	5.0	1.1
1960–69	2.1	4.0	3.3	4.7	5.5	2.1
1970–79	0.8	2.6	2.7	2.6	2.1	1.8
1980–89	0.2	1.8	1.5	1.1	2.2	1.7
1990–99	0.8	1.0	1.8	0.8	-0.2	1.6
2000–09	0.3	0.5	0.3	-0.5	0.0	0.8
2010–19	0.6	0.6	1.1	0.2	0.7	0.5

Source: Bergeaud et al. (2022)

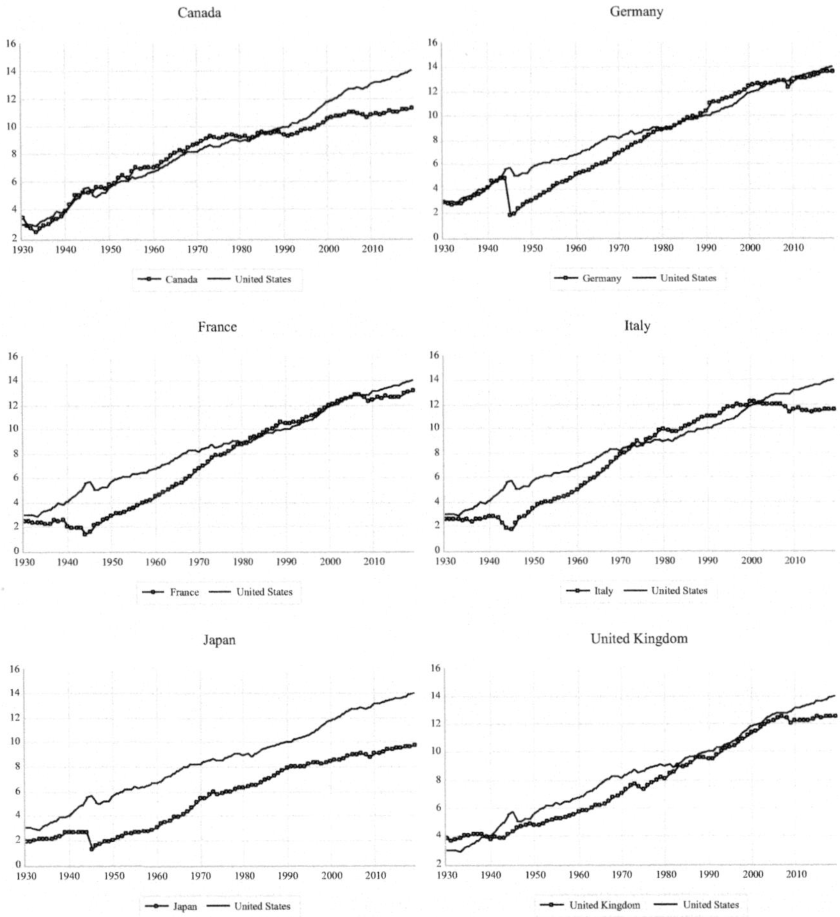

Fig. 6.5 TFP in the US and six other G7 countries, 1930–2019. Source: Bergeaud et al. (2022)

Productivity growth was dismally weak in Italy and Japan after 1990, growth in Japan having come to a halt after the financial crisis of the early 1990s.

Figure 6.5 shows total factor productivity in the US and six other G7 countries from 1930 to 2019. The most noteworthy development is the three continental economies catching up with the US in the postwar decades and then in the case of France, Italy and the UK falling behind after the turn of the century. The catching-up is particularly impressive in Italy and Japan given these countries' war-time destruction, which both destroyed capital and also caused a collapse of productivity. The figure for Japan is similar. There is the collapse at the end of WWII, then a recovery, which is especially strong in the 1960s, then a slowdown after the financial crisis of 1990. Productivity in the UK also converged to the US level in the postwar decades and then lagged behind after the financial crisis in 2008.

Three noteworthy developments are the productivity slowdown in Italy after 1990 and complete stagnation after 1995. This coincides with Italy's adoption of the euro in 1999. While the European single market and the single currency were intended to facilitate convergence between the member countries, the opposite seems to be true from Fig. 6.5 in that total factor productivity continued to grow in Germany while it stagnated in Italy and from around 1995 in France.[8] Second, there is the slowdown of productivity growth in Japan after 1990 following the very rapid growth in the 1950s, the 1960s and 1970s, and a somewhat slower rate in the 1980s. Third, productivity growth in the UK stalls in 2010, and the level of total factor productivity is currently no higher than it was at the beginning of the century.

The stagnation of productivity in the UK since 2010 differs from productivity developments in the 1970s when there was much talk about the UK's bad economic performance. In the 1970s, UK productivity grew at a slower pace than that of the continental European economies while currently it has completely stalled, a development not seen since at least the 1930s, with the accompanying stagnation of average earnings. Crafts and Mills (2020) use long-run data on GDP per hour to estimate trend productivity growth with the Hodrick-Prescott filter. They find that the productivity slowdown in the aftermath of the financial crisis far exceeds any previous slowdown, including the aftermath of the Great Depression (1929), although the rate of labor productivity growth was lower in the late eighteenth century. The suggested causes of the productivity

[8] Giordano and Zollino (2021) study Italian productivity trends back to 1861. They find that a strong TFP growth and expanding manufacturing were the prime drivers of the post - WW II growth and explain the disappointing performance of the Italian economy since 1993 by low productivity growth in the services sector and weak aggreage TFP growth, in addition to subdued capital accumulation.

slowdown include the ebbing away of the ICT boom of the late 1990s and early 2000s, unspecified consequences of the financial crisis and also the effect of Brexit on trade arrangements. The UK seems to suffer from reduced productivity growth in its frontier industries, such as pharmaceuticals, computer software and telecommunications within ICT. Moreover, there is low investment in innovation and skills, both of which contribute to lower growth rates in Eq. (6.13).[9]

There is also a productivity slowdown in Canada over the past 30 years. While productivity growth followed that in the US up to around 1990, it has fallen behind ever since. Andrews et al. (2016) show that this is due to slower rates of innovation in top firms, a decline in the rate of innovation diffusion from the top firms to the rest of the economy, akin to Eq. (6.13) in the Nelson-Phelps model, and lower levels of creative destruction.

We can estimate the Nelson-Phelps relationship, Eq. (6.13), for the four European countries and Japan where the US defines the productivity frontier. Using a fixed-effect estimator, the estimated equation is the following for the 1950–2019 period,

$$\lambda_i = c_i + \underset{(0.8)}{6.1} \log\left(\frac{\Lambda_{US}}{\Lambda_i}\right),$$

where c_i is the country fixed effect for country i and Λ and λ denote the level of productivity and its rate of growth, respectively, as before and the number in parenthesis is the standard error of the estimation. The equation explains almost half of the variation in the growth rate (R-squared is 0.42). The hypothesis that the fixed effects have the same value can be rejected at the 1% level. The hypothesis that the coefficient of the productivity gap is the same cannot be rejected at the 5% level.[10]

The rate of productivity growth λ is measured in percentage points as in Fig. 6.5. The size of the estimated coefficient, 6.1, then implies that a 10% gap between the level of productivity in the US and each of the other five countries, $\log\left(\frac{\Lambda_{US}}{\Lambda_i}\right) = 0.10$, gives productivity growth of 0.6%, a gap of 20% gives growth of 1.2%, and so forth. To take an example, in France

[9] See Coyle and Mei (2023) and Valero and Van Reenen (2019).

[10] When testing for the equality of the five fixed effects, a Wald test gives $F = 24$, while testing for the equality of the five coefficients of the productivity gap gives 0.39.

the value of *log* ($\Lambda_{US}/\Lambda_{FRA}$) was 0.5 in the 1950s and around zero in the 1990s. The equation would then predict that productivity growth fell by 6.1*0.5, or 3.1%, which is similar to the fall in productivity growth shown in Table 6.1.

6.5 Concluding Thoughts

In the post-war world economy, the US has been the engine of growth by pulling productivity growth in other countries and hence real wages. A slowdown of productivity growth in the US then affects the rest of the world. It makes the US a smaller part of the world economy, with geopolitical implications. It slows down real wage growth in the developed world, reducing job satisfaction and increasing disillusionment in governments and the market economy. Increased public debt further aggravates the situation by both crowding out capital at home and abroad, further lowering real wages. The rising public debt triggers capital flows that change net creditor countries, such as the US used to be, into net debtor countries. The difficulties other countries have in generating innovations prevent them from maintaining growth when the gap with the US has shrunk, bringing to an end their golden eras of growth.

References

Ahsan, H., & Haque, M. E. (2017). Threshold effects of human capital: Schooling and economic growth. *Economics Letters, 156*, 48–52.

Andrews, D., Criscuolo, C., & Gal, P. (2016). *The global productivity slowdown, technology divergence and public policy: A firm level perspective*. OECD. https://www.oecd.org/global-forum-productivity/events/GP_Slowdown_Technology_Divergence_and_Public_Policy_Final_after_conference_26_July.pdf

Benhabib, J., & Spiegel, M. M. (1994). The role of human capital in economic development evidence from aggregate cross-country data. *Journal of Monetary Economics, 34*(2), 143–173.

Bergeaud, A., Cette, G., & Lecat, R. (2022, November 24). *The long-term productivity database*. Prod. Bank of France. http://www.longtermproductivity.com/about.html.

Blanchard O. (1985). Debt, deficits, and finite horizons. *Journal of Political Economy, 93*(2), 223–247.

Buiter, W. H. (1981). Time preference and international lending and borrowing in an overlapping-generations model. *Journal of Political Economy, 89*, 769–797.

Buiter, W. H. (1988). Death, birth, productivity growth and debt neutrality. *Economic Journal, 98*(391), 279–293.

Coyle, D., & Mei, J.-C. (2023). Diagnosing the UK productivity slowdown: Which sectors matter and why? *Economica, 90*(359), 813–850.

Crafts, N., & Mills, T. C. (2020). *Is the UK productivity slowdown unprecedented?* University of Sussex. https://sro.sussex.ac.uk/id/eprint/89181/

Fitoussi, J.-P., Jestaz, D., Phelps, E. S., & Zoega, G. (2000). Roots of the recent recoveries: Labor reforms or private sector forces? *Brookings Papers on Economic Activity, 2000*(1), 237–311.

Fitoussi, J.-P., & Phelps, E. S. (1986). Causes of the 1980s slump in Europe. *Brookings Papers on Economic Activity, 1986*(2), 487–520.

Fitoussi J.-P., & Phelps, E. S. (1988). *The Slump in Europe*. Oxford: Blackwell.

Funke, M., Schularick, M., & Trebesch, C. (2016). Going to extremes: Politics after financial crises, 1870-2014. *European Economic Review, 88*, 227–260.

Giordano, C., & Zollino, F. (2021). Long-run factor accumulation and productivity grends in Italy. *Journal of Economic Surveys, 35*(3), 741–803.

Hamada, K., Iwasa, K., & Kikuchi, T. (2009). *Trade and capital movements between countries with different discount rates in a model of perpetual youth*. Manuscript. http://hvar.is/upload/4/SFX/sfx.gif.

Hoon, H. T., & Phelps, E. S. (1992). Macroeconomic shocks in a dynamized model of the natural rate of unemployment. *American Economic Review, 82*(4), 889–900.

Kikuchi, T., & Hamada, K. (2011). Time preference and trade imbalance. *Review of International Economics, 19*(2), 390–401.

Nelson, R. R., & Phelps, E. S. (1966). Investment in humans, technological diffusion, and economic growth. *American Economic Review, 56*(1/2), 69–75.

Phelps, E. S. (1994). *Structural slumps: The modern equilibrium theory of unemployment, interest and assets*. Cambridge, MA: Harvard University Press.

Phelps, E. S. (1999). Behind this structural boom: The role of asset valuations. *American Economic Review: Papers and Proceedings, 89*(2), 63–68.

Rodrik, D. (2021). Why does globalization fuel populism? Economics, culture, and the rise of right-wing populism. *Annual Review of Economics, 13*, 133–170. https://www.annualreviews.org/doi/pdf/10.1146/annurev-economics-070220-032416

Valero, A., & Van Reenen, J. (2019). The UK economy. Centre for Economic Performance. https://cep.lse.ac.uk/pubs/download/EA049.pdf

Vandenbussche, J., Aghion, P., & Meghir, C. (2006). Growth, distance to frontier and composition of human capital. *Journal of Economic Growth, 11*, 97–127.

Weil, P. (1989). Overlapping families of infinitely-lived agents. *Journal of Public Economics, 38*(2), 183–198.

CHAPTER 7

The Pandemic and its Aftermath

We have used data ending in 2019 in previous chapters so as not to allow the effect of the COVID-19 pandemic to influence our results. We now turn to the effects of the pandemic. As of this writing, the economic effects of the pandemic appear to be petering out. Nevertheless, the pandemic has had some persistent effects. The fiscal policy response has caused a large change in the level of public debt, and changes in the organization of work have occurred at rapid speed. We can use our model to show the effect of both developments.

7.1 Higher Public Debt

We start with public debt. Table 7.1 shows central and general government debt as a fraction of GDP for the G7 countries in 2019, 2020, and 2021.

There is a very marked increase in public debt over the three years. Central government debt, which includes the debt of local authorities, has increased by 23.2% of GDP in the UK and general government debt by 24.5% of GDP. In the US, central government debt rose by 21.8% and general government by 19% of GDP. In Europe, central government debt increased by 11.9% in France and general government debt by 15.1%. Debt was already very high in Italy and Japan in 2019, 146% of GDP in Italy and 200.1% in Japan. Central government debt rose by 18.7% in Italy

E. Phelps et al., *The Great Economic Slowdown*,
https://doi.org/10.1007/978-3-031-31441-4_7

Table 7.1 Government debt to GDP (%), G7 countries

	Canada	*France*	*Germany*	*Italy*	*Japan*	*UK*	*US*
Central government debt							
2019	35.7	104.8	43.9	146.0	200.1	109.9	93.1
2020	59.5	123.1	52.5	174.6	221.1	139.3	119.1
2021	54.9	116.7	53.2	164.7	–	133.1	114.9
General government debt							
2019	930.0	123.1	67.7	154.1	225.0	118.5	108.7
2020	126.9	145.7	78.9	183.6	247.8	149.0	134.2
2021	117.3	138.2	77.8	173.7	–	143.0	127.7

Source: OECD

and had risen by 21.1% in 2020 in Japan. For general government debt the changes were 19% for Italy and 22.8% for Japan.

Figure 7.1 shows central government debt as a fraction of GDP for six G7 countries since 2000. Note the upward trend in all countries except for Germany where debt fell between 2010 and 2019 after the financial crisis.

The effect of the increased public debt should be as described in the previous chapters. In the one-sector model from Chap. 2, the increased debt raises the equilibrium real rate of interest and crowds out the capital stock by creating a wedge between household wealth and the capital stock. The increase in real interest rates is larger when the sum of the elasticities of the demand for capital and the supply of wealth with respect to the real interest rate is low. But, as described in that chapter, the size of the stock of public debt relative to total nonhuman wealth also matters. As the size of the public debt rises, which was the case in most countries before COVID, then each percentage increase in the stock of public debt has a larger proportionate impact on the real interest rate.

In the two-sector model from Chap. 3, where both labor and capital are used in the production of the consumer good, the effect of the increased stock of public debt is to increase consumption demand causing the real rate of interest to rise and the shadow price of capital to fall. This then causes the stock of capital to fall as in the one-sector model. In the two-country model from Chap. 6, the effect is to increase the world real rate of interest, reduce the capital stock in both countries, increase (perceived) wealth in the debtor country, and increase the net foreign assets of the creditor country.

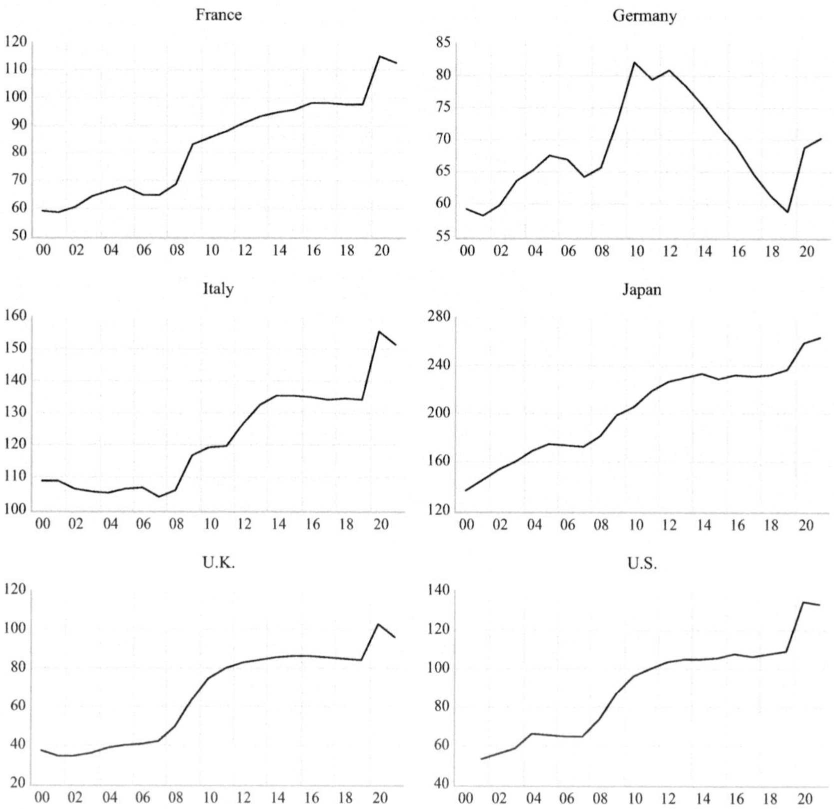

Fig. 7.1 General government debt as a ratio to GDP (%). Source: OECD

Finally, the level of markups is affected as described in Chap. 4. A rise in wealth, by creating a wedge between the total demand for capital and customers, on the one hand, and the supply of wealth, on the other hand, raises the real rate of interest and lowers both the shadow price of capital and the shadow price of customers. The lower shadow price of customers makes it optimal for firms to raise markups, which makes the shadow price of capital fall further, reducing the capital stock even more.

7.2 Working From Home

There is a second effect of COVID-19 operating through the reorganization of work. We can show the macroeconomic effect using our one-sector model from Chap. 2. Assuming that working from home and working in the office are perfect substitutes, the introduction of new connective technologies (such as Zoom or Teams), which enable workers to work from home for part of the week, has the effect of increasing the stock of productive capital (from $\tilde{k}$ to $\tilde{k}+\sigma\frac{\tilde{S}}{\overline{L}}$ where σ denotes the share of homes being used as a workplace and $\tilde{S}\equiv\frac{S}{\Lambda}$).

Output per unit of effective labor is now a function of both capital $\tilde{k}\equiv K/\left(\Lambda N\overline{L}\right)$ and housing $\tilde{S}\equiv S/\Lambda$, since S is defined in per capita terms:

$$Y/\left(\Lambda N\overline{L}\right)=f\left(\tilde{k}+\sigma\frac{\tilde{S}}{\overline{L}}\right)$$

The profit-maximizing conditions for capital and labor from Chap. 2 can be rewritten as

$$r=f'\left(\tilde{k}+\sigma\frac{\tilde{S}}{\overline{L}}\right)-\delta \text{ and} \tag{2.7'}$$

$$\tilde{v}=f\left(\tilde{k}+\sigma\frac{\tilde{S}}{\overline{L}}\right)-\left(\tilde{k}+\sigma\frac{\tilde{S}}{\overline{L}}\right)f'\left(\tilde{k}+\sigma\frac{\tilde{S}}{\overline{L}}\right), \tag{2.8'}$$

and the demand for aggregate capital can be derived by inverting Eq. (2.7')

$$\tilde{k}+\sigma\frac{\tilde{S}}{\overline{L}}=\mu(r);\mu'(r)<0. \tag{2.12'}$$

This equation can be rewritten as

$$\frac{K}{\Lambda N}+\tilde{S}=\mu(r)\overline{L}+(1-\sigma)\tilde{S};\mu'(r)<0. \tag{2.13'}$$

This equation gives a downward-sloping demand for aggregate capital schedule. While this equation shows that $\tilde{k}$ is inversely related to *r*, it remains to show that $\frac{K}{\Lambda N}+\tilde{S}$ is also inversely related to *r*. Equation (2.19) in Chap. 2 had the marginal rate of substitution between consumption of the nondurable good and the housing stock equal to the sum of the real interest rate and the rate of depreciation. Using the Blanchard-Buiter-Weil consumption function and noting that $W = (K/N) + S$, we obtained

$$(\theta+\rho)\left[1+\frac{(K/N)/\Lambda}{S/\Lambda}+\frac{\tilde{v}\bar{L}}{(r-\lambda+\theta)(S/\Lambda)}\right]=r+\delta, \qquad (2.20)$$

where $\tilde{v}$ is normalized wages. Now, using the unchanged factor-price frontier, Eq. (2.9) in Chap. 2, and Eq. (2.13') in Eq. (2.20), we get

$$(\theta+\rho)\left[1-\sigma+\frac{\mu(r)\bar{L}}{S/\Lambda}+\frac{\phi(r)\bar{L}}{(r-\lambda+\theta)(S/\Lambda)}\right]=r+\delta \qquad (2.21')$$

by dividing both sides of Eq. (2.13') by $\tilde{S}$ and substituting for the second term in the square bracket in Eq. (2.20). This goes to show that the demand for aggregate capital $\frac{K}{\Lambda N}+\tilde{S}$ is negatively related to the real interest rate, as in Eq. (2.22) in Chap. 2.

The upward-sloping supply of wealth curve is unchanged from Chap. 2. The equilibrium real interest rate is then determined by the intersection of the demand for capital curve, Eq. (2.13') and the unchanged supply of wealth curve, Eq. (2.10) in Chap. 2.

We can now derive the effect of the introduction of connective technologies, which are measured by the fraction σ of homes used for working. Before the advent of these technologies σ was equal to zero but now becomes a positive number between zero and one (Fig. 7.2).

Starting with the first effect, from Eq. (2.13') we see that a rise of σ makes the demand for the aggregate capital $\left(\frac{S}{\Lambda}+\tilde{k}\bar{L}\right)$ curve shift to the

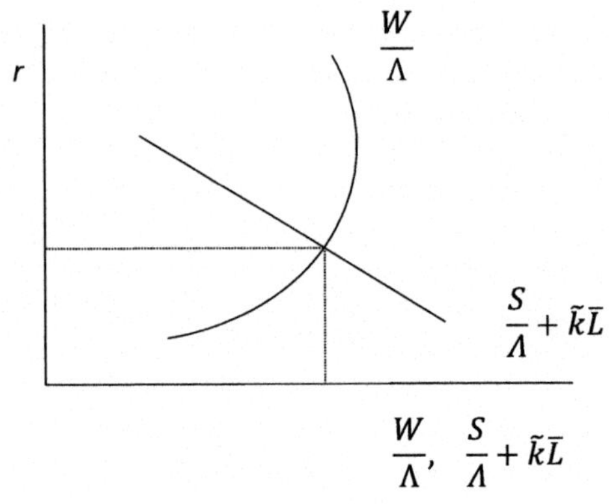

Fig. 7.2 Capital market equilibrium with connective technologies

left.[1] Intuitively, when workers start to work from home there is less need for office space. This effect may be described as a helicopter drop of capital in the form of homes partially converted to a workplace.

There is a second effect. The connective technologies save commuting time, which increases both leisure and hours of work. A rise in hours worked $\bar{L}$ increases the demand for capital, making $\tilde{k}_{\text{new}} + \sigma \frac{\tilde{S}}{\bar{L}} > \tilde{k}_{\text{old}}$ for an unchanged real rate of interest since $\bar{L}_{\text{new}} > \bar{L}_{\text{old}}$.

The third effect is the increased labor productivity that comes from the new technologies, as shown by Gordon and Sayed (2022) in industries using connective technologies in the post-COVID period, and Bloom et al. (2022) who find that "hybrid working from home" increases worker retention, job satisfaction, and productivity. This effect shows up in an increase of Λ, which in a new steady state does not affect the normalized levels of capital, nor the real rate, but raises real wages, aggregate output, and consumption, in effect the size of the economy.

There remains to describe the effect of the new technologies on factor prices. The first effect of connective technologies reduces the demand for capital $\tilde{k}$ and hence the equilibrium real rate of interest. The fall in interest rates then has the effect of lowering the rental on housing, prompting people to move into larger houses $\tilde{S}$. The net effect is for workers to live in larger apartments and houses, for firms to use less capital $\tilde{k}$, and for real interest rates to be lower. The effect on real wages will then depend on

[1] Eberly et al. (2021) refer to the use of homes in the production of output as "potential capital."

whether firms' use of capital—which includes workers' homes $\tilde{k}+\sigma\frac{\tilde{S}}{\overline{L}}$ — is different from their use of capital before $\tilde{k}$. If the use of total capital is increased $\tilde{k}_{\text{new}}+\sigma\frac{\tilde{S}}{\overline{L}}>\tilde{k}_{\text{old}}$ then the real wage will rise, but if it is decreased, the real wage will fall. The second effect tells us that the use of total capital is increased. The connective technologies save commuting time, which increases hours of work making $\tilde{k}_{\text{new}}+\sigma\frac{\tilde{S}}{\overline{L}}>\tilde{k}_{\text{old}}$.

References

Bloom, N., Han, R., & Liang, J. (2022). *How hybrid working from home works out.* NBER Working Paper 30292.

Eberly, J. C., Haskel, J., & Mizen, P. (2021). *"Potential capital", working from home, and economic resilience.* NBER Working Paper 29431.

Gordon, R. J., & Sayed, H. (2022). *A new interpretation of productivity growth dynamics in the pre-pandemic and pandemic era U.S. economy, 1950–2022.* NBER Working Paper 30267.

CHAPTER 8

Growth to the Rescue

In this book, we have focused on the consequences of the slowdown in productivity growth starting in the early 1970s. As regards future growth of productivity, there are, fortunately, some reasons to be optimistic. Brynjolfsson and McAfee (2017) argue that progress in digital technology is driving productivity growth and will create valuable jobs in the future. While employment may suffer in the short term, growth and employment will benefit in the longer term, with organizational innovation and enhanced human capital. Moreover, as is described in our recent book, *Dynamism*, robots may both replace workers and increase their productivity.

Brynjolfsson et al. (2017) explain the contrast between the slowdown in measured productivity growth that comes from national accounts data and the advent of new promising technologies, especially artificial intelligence, by an implementation lag, which consists of the time between the discovery of new technologies and the time when the necessary investment has been made and institutional changes have taken place. They make the case that technologies such as self-driving cars will free up millions of workers in the US who are currently employed as truck drivers and taxi drivers, as well as increasing the utilization of cars used in private transport by enabling people to share private cars.

There are signs that productivity in the industries using the new connective technologies is starting to grow more rapidly. Gordon and Sayed (2022) separate work-from-home service industries from contact

E. Phelps et al., *The Great Economic Slowdown*,
https://doi.org/10.1007/978-3-031-31441-4_8

industries and find that the rate of labor productivity growth in the former has increased in the post-COVID period, 2021–2022. They find that while productivity growth post- pandemic is similar to the pre-pandemic one, productivity growth in the work-from-home industries is rising at a rate of 3.1%, which reflects the influence of the new connective technologies. However, the new technologies have yet to raise overall productivity growth by much.

There are two main reasons why technological innovations may affect productivity growth with a lag. First, technological innovations take a long time to be implemented through a series of microinventions (see Mokyr, 1993). Macroinventions are radical breakthroughs that create entire new industries, while microinventions consist of incremental improvements, which are often necessary to bring a macroinvention to its full potential. The stream of macroinventions continues, for example, in the form of artificial intelligence in the workplace and the increasing concentration of tasks that can be performed in mobile phones. These macroinventions can be expected to gradually increase the rate of measured productivity growth.

Second, new technologies affect the evolution of institutions, as is described by Eggertsson (2005). The lag between the invention of new technology and its application may be long, owing to a long learning process and adjustment costs, the latter taking the form of reorganization of industry in terms of location and networks. Thus it took about half a century of innovations and costly investment before electricity had made its full impact on productivity in the US. The replacement of water and steam power by electricity required the reorganization of the production process when each factory acquired its own electrical motors. Crafts (2004) finds that steam had its peak impact about a hundred years after its invention. Technology may also gradually affect the institutions of the economy and the political system, but this may take quite a long time.

Our models can be used to show the economic effects of an expected future rebound of productivity growth. Expectations of faster productivity growth would make workers anticipate more rapidly growing wages, and their stock of human capital would jump, increasing consumption and decreasing saving. This would then have the effect of raising the real rate of interest, which would lower stock prices (the shadow price of capital) and reduce the use of capital (normalized by productivity) in production. The effect of stronger anticipated productivity growth on housing demand reinforces this effect. When consumption increases, demand for housing also increases, which makes the real rate of interest rise further through stronger demand for productive capital because more capital has been converted for residential uses, less for use as office space. Because of reduced wealth and consumption caused by lower stock prices, firms would lower markups, which would reduce the share of profits in GDP. There is also a positive effect on employment working through an increase in labor demand, which increases the opportunity cost of leisure, making people work more.

A faster rate of productivity growth in the US would affect the rest of the world. Reduced saving in the US would have the effect of raising world interest rates and lowering stock markets around the world. With reduced use of capital, wages would fall but then increase more rapidly than before, owing to faster productivity growth. The productivity gap between the US and China and other countries would widen, and China would become a relatively smaller part of the world economy. Geopolitical tensions could be reduced.

The return to a period of more rapid productivity growth in the West will alleviate many of the macroeconomic and political problems faced by the US, the West, and the world as a whole. A return to faster growth of productivity would make wages rise faster, real interest rates rise, the stock market come down from its current high levels, making the wealth distribution more equal, prompting people to move to larger homes, and lowering the share of profits in GDP. At the geopolitical level, the West would be less challenged or threatened by a resurgent China. The innovative technologies used in our daily lives will then provide a solution to many of the world's problems.

References

Brynjolfsson, E., & Mitchell, T. (2017). What can machine learning do? Workforce implications. *Science, 358*(6370), 1530–1534.

Crafts, N. (2004). Steam as a general purpose technology: A growth accounting perspective. *Economic Journal, 114*(495), 338–351.

Eggertsson, T. (2005). *Imperfect institutions: Possibilities and limits of reform.* Ann Arbor, MI: University of Michigan Press.

Gordon, R. J., & Sayed, H. (2022). *A new interpretation of productivity growth dynamics in the pre-pandemic and pandemic era U.S. economy, 1950–2022.* NBER Working Paper 30267.

Mokyr, J. (1993). *The new economic history and the industrial revolution.* Boulder, CO: Westview Press.

CHAPTER 9

Economic Policies

It remains to discuss our policy advice. How do the policies that follow our analysis differ from mainstream policies, that is, those practiced by the West in recent decades?

Our analysis of the causes of the problems facing the West in recent years lays the blame on the structure of the economy and its inability to innovate. The problems are found on the supply side of the economy; they are nonmonetary and cannot be addressed through conventional fiscal and monetary policies. Although the public sector, rules and regulations, and the laws of the land reflect economic policies, these are a part of the structure of the economy. The structure affects incentives and decisions made by firms and households.

In our view, what matters most is the long-term trend of the economy. A good economy is one where people have expanding opportunities to take part, opportunities for personal growth through participation in the economy, and opportunities to experience rising wages over time. Work is a source of life satisfaction, and here the satisfaction from having a job plays a key role. For the population to flourish, the economy must generate innovations, not just to make increased production and higher wages possible but to generate interesting jobs where such innovations and discoveries are made.

While many can profit from seeking rent at the expense of others, such rent-seeking activities are not a part of our good economy. They divert

E. Phelps et al., *The Great Economic Slowdown*,
https://doi.org/10.1007/978-3-031-31441-4_9

workers' time and ingenuity from discoveries that benefit all to merely reshuffling the chairs on the deck, making some rich at the expense of others. As the late economist William Baumol emphasized, all countries have ambitious individuals, but the structure of the economy—to use our terminology—determines how they spend their time, whether they enrich or impoverish their countries or, at best, make no difference one way or the other.[1] By comparing the fortunes of different countries' wealthiest individuals in terms of how they amassed their fortune, we can see what distinguishes the countries. While in some countries these individuals enriched themselves through botched privatizations of public utilities or state-owned enterprises, in others it was through path-breaking innovations that have transformed our economies. It should not come as a surprise that the latter countries belong to the West, where societies are built on the rule of law and where corruption, although always present, is less destructive.

9.1 The Current Morass

Before discussing our policy recommendations, let us start by taking a look at mainstream macroeconomic thought and its policy recommendations. The beginning of this century saw the advent of what became known as the Great Moderation. Mainstream Keynesian—or New Keynesian—economics had supposedly reached the stage at which the business cycle could be made smoother and inflation kept on target. When the economy contracted and inflation fell below target, central banks could lower interest rates to stimulate the economy, and if this turned out to be insufficient, governments could step in and increase expenditures or cut taxes. It did not matter much which taxes were cut or which expenditures increased, the mantra is the size of the multiplier, an idea going back to Robert Malthus.

Our departure from the recent mainstream can be framed in the anthropological account by Axel Leijonhufvud of economics in the early 1970s as consisting of the macro and the micro castes. While the macro caste recommends inflating when inflation is below a target and deflating when it is above the target, the micro caste would point at the effects on decisions by households and firms. A prolonged attempt to inflate the American

[1] Baumol (1990).

economy following the bursting of the dot-com bubble and the September 11 attacks spurred increased risk-taking in the financial sector. The consequence was a house-price bubble financed through the issuance of mortgage-backed securities that became worthless, which paralyzed the banking system in the West in the fall of 2008. The response consisted of drastic interest rate cuts and deficit spending. The macro caste discussed how nominal interest rates could be made to be negative by abolishing cash and making all money electronic. Only with negative nominal interest rates could the economy be sufficiently inflated.[2] The low dollar interest rates have increased dollar debt around the world in the years that followed, including in emerging economies, setting the stage for another financial crisis when US interest rates are increased again, as is currently underway. Deficit spending was used to complement monetary policy, and the main concern was to find ways to spend the money: it was the level of spending rather than the economy's structure that was prioritized.

The consequences of the expansionary policy of the past 14 years are now becoming apparent. The stimulus—increased further to combat the economic effects of COVID—has run into supply constraints. Many workers have decided to withdraw from the labor force, to enjoy early retirement, and cash in on the asset price bubbles fueled by the monetary stimulus. After all, it is the productive resources of the economy and the level of technology that determine output and the standard of living. The fiscal deficits have also gradually made the stock of public debt increase, which constitutes unproductive wealth.

9.2 The Many Pitfalls of the Two Mainstream Policies

Today's policy-makers have been raised on one or the other of two extant bodies of economic theory: the Keynesian and the neoclassical.

The Keynesian Influence

The application of Keynesian remedies to the Great Slowdown has many pitfalls. Keynesian stimulus is not well suited to accelerating the pace of innovations and productivity growth. Instead, it ends up running into supply constraints, inflation, and asset price bubbles. Policy makers also

[2] See Lilley and Rogoff (2020).

run into the problem of time inconsistency when the short-term remedies of monetary and fiscal expansion create future problems. Monetary stimulus contributes to a larger stock of corporate and government debt, at home and abroad, and fiscal deficits cause the accumulation of public debt. In our models, the stock of public debt has the effect of raising the equilibrium real rate of interest and reducing the stock of productive capital. Finally, there is the problem of international coordination. Fiscal deficits in one country gradually raise the world real rate of interest through a higher stock of debt, which crowds out capital and raises the marginal product of capital. We showed in Chap. 5 how government deficits in the US have the effect of raising the world real rate of interest and reducing the stock of productive capital in other countries. In Chap. 1, we showed how higher interest rates lower employment by reducing real wages relative to household nonwage income. We also showed how the higher real rates of interest have the effect of reducing the housing stock through higher rentals.

Recently, Blanchard (2019) argued that fiscal deficits and debt may have only limited fiscal costs due to low interest rates. Furman and Summers (2020) argued in a similar vein that, in a world of cheap capital, concerns about crowding out of private investment are not important. This stands in contrast to a long history of economic thought going back to David Ricardo, leading up to Modigliani and Phelps, where deficit financing of public expenditures set back the growth of capital. Blanchard, Furman, and Summers argue that the reduction of the capital stock does not affect output much if the real rate of interest is close to zero; the economy is in a Ramseyan steady state with a low or zero rate of productivity growth. Furthermore, Furman and Summers argue that debt-to-GDP ratios are a misleading measure of fiscal sustainability and should be replaced by a comparison of interest payment flows and GDP flows. Others have disagreed, such as Boskin (2020), who argues that an increase in the debt ratio could lead to higher taxes, higher interest rates, weaker growth, and increased intergenerational inequity.

In our model in Chap. 1, we found that the state of low real rates of interest is no guarantee that public debt will not have a negative effect on the stock of capital, output, and consumption. An increase in the stock of debt raises the equilibrium real rate of interest, to an increasing degree as the level of debt rises. The magnitude of the increase then depends on the sensitivity of the supply of wealth by households and the demand for capital by firms on the real rate of interest. Moreover, in Chap. 4 we found that even when the real rate of interest is low, the marginal product of capital is higher because imperfect competition in the goods market generates positive markups of price over marginal cost. Higher markups have the effect of increasing the divergence between the rental of capital and the return on capital, creating the illusion of dynamic inefficiency, when in fact the capital stock is below the golden rule level. It follows that a fall in the stock of capital lowers output and consumption even when the real rate of interest is close to zero.

The Neoclassical Influence

We are left with the neoclassical school of thought, which is the foundation of existing supply-side economics. According to this school, low personal income taxes and low corporate taxes are conducive to economic growth by affecting incentives to work and to invest as discussed by Mundell (1971). But some innovative economies have large public sectors and high taxes, while others have small public sectors and low taxes. The economies of the high-tax countries Denmark, Finland, and Sweden are —or were, as the case may be—very innovative despite the high tax rates. In the US, the state of California has both high state income tax rates and a very innovative economy.

Moreover, the adoption of measures believed to have a basis in neoclassical theory also has pitfalls. The deep slash of tax rates on corporate profits obtained by the Trump administration in 2017 has yet to galvanize innovation and growth in America.

The Source of Satisfaction

A different thesis is that utility stems from consumption and leisure, as assumed in the real business cycle school. Instead, in our view, happiness stems to some extent from job satisfaction; that is, the availability of challenging and rewarding jobs. As is explained in Phelps' book *Mass Flourishing*, as well as in our recent book *Dynamism*, the degree of importance that people place on exercising their creativity, on meeting challenges posed by their jobs, and having the occasional opportunity to express some independence in their work is likely to be crucial for the generation of a highly rewarding economy. Phelps maintains that in the great era of widespread innovation, from as early as the late 1870s to the early 1970s, many fortunate participants drew as much satisfaction from their engagement in their work than from their pecuniary gains.

9.3 Policies to Spur Innovation

What institutions appear to matter for economic performance? There are many institutions that can either obstruct or encourage innovation. It is reasonable to hypothesize that organized stock exchanges, angel investors, company law, suitable bankruptcy provisions, and corporate governance foster innovative activities. General institutions such as the rule of law and the protection of property rights, as well as the provision of enough personal and national security to safeguard earnings, saving, and investment are needed for any market economy. However, they are not sufficient to generate dynamism.

Many of the corporatist institutions that enable employees, unions, local communities, and other interests to veto, block, or limit entrepreneurial ventures and shifts in corporate operations may choke off valuable innovation. Bureaucratic "red tape" and employment protection legislation are two such corporatist institutions. Red tape is a measure of the volume of required licenses, hindering or deterring the establishment of new firms and new projects. Similarly, a small share of workers with tertiary education makes innovation difficult because the required skilled workforce is not readily available. Applying the insights of Nelson and Phelps, research has found that tertiary education becomes more important as an economy approaches the productivity frontier, and innovations become more important for growth.[3]

We have hypothesized that differences in culture, even among the developed OECD economies, may help explain some of the intercountry differences in innovation and economic growth.[4] Some observers have suggested that European schooling drains children of some of their playfulness and their desire to create. The national culture has effectively meant sheltering older and more established institutions and interests from competition, which may impede innovations that upset the established order. Critics say that these seeming deficiencies are not causes—they are effects of ill-chosen institutions. But what are the causes of the

[3] See Vandenbussche et al. (2004).

[4] See Phelps (2013) and Phelps et al. (2020).

institutions, if not the prevailing political economy—the public policies—on which culture may have much influence?

"Young America," as Abraham Lincoln said in his lecture on Discoveries and Inventions, "has a great passion—a perfect rage—for the new."[5] Yet America is not young anymore. In the past five decades much of the West has become more stagnant every year. We would call for a renewed commitment to liberal education that instills a sense of adventure in children and young adults. In the long run, the future of the West will hinge on our ability to restore to society the modern values that fueled innovation of the West—values such as individualism, vitalism, and self-expression.

References

Abraham, L. (1859, February 11). *Second lecture on discoveries and inventions.*

Baumol, W. (1990). Entrepreneurship: Productive, unproductive, and destructive. *Journal of Political Economy, 98*(1), 893–921.

Blanchard, O. (2019). Public debt and Low interest rates. *American Economic Review, 109*(4), 197–229.

Boskin, M. J. (2020). Are large deficits and debt dangerous? *American Economic Review: Papers and Proceedings, 110*, 145–148.

Furman, J., & Summers, L. (2020). *A reconsideration of fiscal policy in the era of low interest rates.* Brookings Institution. furman-summers-fiscal-reconsideration-discussion-draft.pdf.

Lilley, A., & Rogoff, K. (2020). *Negative interest rate policy in the post COVID-19 world.* CEPR. VoxEu. voxeu.org.

Mundell, R. A. (1971). *The dollar and the policy mix: 1971.* International Finance Section. Princeton University.

Phelps, E. S. (2013). *Mass flourishing: How grassroots innovation created jobs, challenge, and change.* Princeton, NJ: Princeton University Press.

Phelps, E. S., Bojilov, R., Teck Hoon, H., & Zoega, G. (2020). *Dynamism: The values that drive innovation, job satisfaction, and economic growth.* Cambridge, MA: Harvard University Press.

Vandenbussche, J., Aghion, P., & Meghir, C. (2004). Growth, distance to frontier and composition of human capital. *Journal of Economic Growth, 11*(2), 97–127. Accessed May 11, 2022, from. https://doi.org/10.1007/s10887-006-9002-y

[5] Abraham (1859).

CHAPTER 10

Summary and Outstanding Issues

In this book we have described how the slowdown of productivity growth, starting in the early 1980s, has contributed to a falling equilibrium real rate of interest, a booming stock market, slowing wage growth and a rising share of profits in national income.

Another adverse effect is the increase in public debt, which, in creating a wedge between household wealth and capital, crowds out the capital stock. In line with the golden rule literature, the crowding out of capital can reduce output and consumption even when real interest rates are low in imperfectly competitive goods markets where markups create a wedge between the net marginal product of capital and the real rate of interest.

In a two-sector model, the slowdown of productivity growth raises the value of capital by lowering real interest rates and raising markups of price over marginal cost in a customer market model. The fall in population growth has a similar effect. Both lower expected productivity growth and a lower rate of population growth have the effect of lowering the value of a larger market share, thus making firms raise markups of price over marginal cost. Increased public debt also lowers the value of a customer by raising the real rate of interest and increases current demand, which makes markups go up. It follows that increased public debt, lower productivity growth and lower population growth all make firms raise markups and the share of profits in national income rise as a consequence. This is consistent

E. Phelps et al., *The Great Economic Slowdown*,
https://doi.org/10.1007/978-3-031-31441-4_10

with the stylized facts of a booming stock market and a rising share of profits in national income observed in the US.

In a two-country model, a slowdown of productivity growth in the leading economy affects the rest of the world, slowing down real wage growth. Increased public debt further aggravates the situation by both crowding out capital at home and abroad, further lowering real wages. The rising public debt triggers capital flows that change net creditor countries, such as the US used to be, into net debtor countries.

There are many institutions that can either obstruct or encourage innovation. It may be that the internal forces that were so powerful over the many years of unprecedented innovation—societal values such as the desire for self-expression—had weakened in one country after another by the early 1970s. An innovative capitalist system requires a well-developed stock market, investors, company law, bankruptcy provisions, and good corporate governance. General institutions such as the rule of law, the protection of property rights, and a noncorrupt public sector provide the basis for a well-functioning market economy. However, they are not sufficient to generate dynamism. In contrast, many of the corporatist institutions that enable employees and unions and other interests to limit entrepreneurial ventures and shifts in corporate operations may choke off valuable innovation.

Although this book ends here, there are factors we have not included here such as tax rates. There is still much research to be done.

Index[1]

[1] Note: Page numbers followed by 'n' refer to notes.

E. Phelps et al., *The Great Economic Slowdown*,
https://doi.org/10.1007/978-3-031-31441-4